GRANT'S KEEPER

The Life of John A. Rawlins

J. C. Ladenheim

HERITAGE BOOKS
2011

HERITAGE BOOKS
AN IMPRINT OF HERITAGE BOOKS, INC.

Books, CDs, and more—Worldwide

For our listing of thousands of titles see our website at
www.HeritageBooks.com

Published 2011 by
HERITAGE BOOKS, INC.
Publishing Division
100 Railroad Ave. #104
Westminster, Maryland 21157

Copyright © 2011 Jules C. Ladenheim

Other books by the author:
Abe Lincoln Afloat
Alien Horseman: An Italian Shavetail with Custer
Custer's Thorn: The Life of Frederick W. Benteen
The Jarrett-Palmer Express of 1876: Coast to Coast in Eighty-three Hours
Lincoln and Emancipation in the District of Columbia

All rights reserved. No part of this book may be reproduced or transmitted in any form or by any means, electronic or mechanical, including photocopying, recording or by any information storage and retrieval system without written permission from the author, except for the inclusion of brief quotations in a review.

International Standard Book Numbers
Paperbound: 978-0-7884-5333-5
Clothbound: 978-0-7884-8791-0

I don't need a brilliant staff,
I want a loyal one.

—*General George S. Patton, Jr.*

CONTENTS

INTRODUCTION vii
EARLY YEARS 1
WAR IN THE WEST 27
WAR IN THE EAST 125
FINAL DAYS 193
NOTES 223
BIBLIOGRAPHY 245
INDEX 257

INTRODUCTION

When Grant went off to the War in 1861, there were few, if any, who believed he would succeed. The Governor of Illinois did not believe in him; he delayed a colonel's commission until he had no one else to appoint. His family did not believe in him; it would not even advance him the price of a uniform. His wife did not believe in him; she made him take along his son, to discourage his alcohol temptation. Grant did not believe in himself; he sent for a young, passionate, resolute Galena lawyer, named John A. Rawlins, who he thought would keep him out of trouble.

This is the story of John Rawlins, the man who guarded Grant, reproached him, idolized him, loved him. What he did and what Grant accomplished are inextricably bound together. Without him, many doubt that Grant could have fulfilled his destiny as a distinguished military commander. One slip brought to public attention might have ended his career. Many malignant forces kept watch on Grant, knowing of his disability and waiting for him to succumb.

Some believe that Grant's affliction was negligible; that Rawlins exaggerated it, to bolster his self importance. In the thirty-nine articles about Grant and alcohol,[1] more than a few support this premise.

Rawlins was not a mere nursery maid, but a trusted confidant, advisor and critic. As one of his staff wrote:

> The two together constituted a military character of great simplicity, force and singleness of purpose which has passed into history under the name of Grant.[2]

The full story of Grant and his affliction could not be disclosed until after his death in 1885. Even then, his wife objected to the disclosure of documents alluding to his alcohol affliction.[3] Small wonder that the reminiscences of Wilson, Dana and Cadwallader were not published in Grant's lifetime. Others in the inner circle were also reticent to address the subject, in deference to Grant's public image. Moreover, the escalation of the great temperance movements in the latter half of the nineteenth century affixed to alcohol dependence an implacable moral stigma. Those who believe that Grant's dependence detracts from his reputation should be asked if the fame of a gold-medal runner diminishes, if it is learned that he ran with a lame foot.

The services of John A. Rawlins were recognized during his short life and subsequently for a few decades. Thereafter, his memory was subsumed into an adored detoxified image of the great Union general. But Dr. John Brinton, Grant's chief medical officer at Cairo, Illinois, has left us with an appreciation of his services:

> He [Rawlins] was a most extraordinary man, and by his faithfulness toward the General, his good judgment, his fearless and outspoken expression of his convictions, and his quick sense of right and wrong greatly assisted his chief in arriving at just conclusions, and in withstanding the temptations by which he was surrounded.[4]

To make the study more meaningful, the author has included a brief outline of the battles in which Grant participated, together with a few semi-diagrammatic maps to supplement the descriptions. Often, the names of the division and corps commanders have been omitted, where the names do not advance the narrative. The omissions are in no way intended to demean their services.

During the preparation of this study, I have had the privilege of using the facilities of the Library of Congress; the National Archives; the New York Public Library; the Newark, New Jersey, Public Library; the Goshen, New York, Public Library; the Danbury, Connecticut, Public Library; the Galena,

Illinois, Public Library; and the Cheyenne, Wyoming Historical Society. I wish to thank Steve Repp, curator of the Alfred Muller Collection, for permission to use the photographs entrusted to his care and for his informative tour of Galena. Elsa Jablonsky was kind enough to help me obtain photographs of the Rawlins statue. To Steve Pisani, I express my thanks for reviewing the study and for his learned and valuable comments. I regret that not all could be included in the text. Peter Russell of Kent, England provided innumerable and salient corrections and greatly contributed to my knowledge of the Rawlins family. Bernice Bertram of the Teaneck Public Library was most helpful, as was Mrs. Jean Ganley, my secretary. To my editor, Debbie Riley, I express my deep appreciation.

EARLY DAYS

In the early nineteenth century, a well-trod pathway for westward emigration led from Virginia into Tennessee and Kentucky; and from there over the Ohio River into the Northwest Territory, or across the Mississippi River into Missouri.

James Dawson Rawlins, the father of the subject of our study, was born in Clark County, Kentucky on February 28, 1801, and at the age of eighteen, moved from Madison County, Kentucky to Howard County, Missouri. On September 14, 1827 he migrated to Galena in Jo Daviess County[5] in northwest Illinois, later known as "the lead mine district." The town was situated two miles from the mouth of the Galena River, where it empties into the Mississippi. The river is narrow but deep, navigable in all seasons for steamboats. At the time when James first arrived, Galena had but three cabins, a few smelting furnaces, a trading house[6] and several taverns. On October 5, 1828, he returned to Missouri to marry the twenty-five year old Lovisa Collier;[7] the daughter of an old

Indian fighter of Kentucky stock. The census of 1830 records that James Rollins owned a female slave, who may have come with Lovisa's dowry or may have been on loan. A son, Jarrard Owen, was born to them during their stay in Missouri.

The family returned to Illinois around 1831. James Rawlins drove teams between Galena and Mineral Point, Wisconsin. During the Black Hawk War in the summer of 1832, he witnessed several skirmishes between the militia and the Indians and was sufficiently close to hear the whine of the bullets. The conflict was waged against the Sauk and Fox tribes, who had returned to Illinois to reclaim the land from which they had been driven. In 1834, the couple moved to Guilford, six miles from Galena, where he put down a deposit on 320 acres of homestead land of grassland and trees. James tilled a few acres, wagoned and later became a charcoal burner. Their first child, Jarrard, was succeeded on February 13, 1831 by John Aaron, the next oldest. Seven other children followed, all but one, boys. The family surname was early listed in the census as "Rollins," later changed to "Rawlins."

When news of the discovery of gold in California reached the East, James and his eldest son, Jarrard, left the homestead in 1849 and set out with ox cart to seek their fortune. John, then eighteen years old, was left in charge and struggled to support the family. The father returned after three years (his obituary said he was away only six months[8]), but Jarrard remained in California. He obtained employment with the revenue service and died in 1869.[9]

James, the father, was somewhat indolent, confining his labor to the management of his small farm plot. Perhaps he was a heavy drinker, judging from his son's implacable antipathy to alcohol,[10] although this seems unlikely, since the man lived to the age of ninety-one. The mother, about whom not much is known, was a firm and loving woman, said to be well-versed in medicinal herbs and nursing skills. She successfully reared her nine children in accordance with the strictest moral principles and lived long enough (1803-1891) to see all her surviving children attain an honorable station in life.[11] A devout Methodist, she believed John Aaron to be suited to the ministry.

John and his brothers earned most of their livelihood from charcoal burning. At the time, a lead mining boom was underway. Sixty square miles of lead deposits extended from northwest Illinois into Wisconsin and Missouri.[12] Galena was the center of the lead mining industry. The town was named for galena, a natural form of lead sulfide. Indians smelted this mineral in crude furnaces and used it for body and face paint. In 1690 fur trappers reported seeing the mineral. By the mid nineteenth century Jo Daviess County was producing eighty percent of the lead mined in the United States; and, in consequence, Galena grew in importance as a commercial center for the upper Mississippi basin, even surpassing Chicago by 1855 in the wholesale business.[13] As a river port, Galena conducted a lively shipping business with the Mississippi towns, especially St. Louis.

One of the important requirements of lead smelting is charcoal, which was used to raise the temperature of the lead smelting furnace to 1000 degrees Fahrenheit. Charcoal manufacture requires long hours of diligent attention and much back breaking labor.

In brief, this is the process: Hardwood is harvested and trimmed to eighteen inch sticks. A circular area of clay soil is leveled, and on it the wood is carefully stacked in the shape of an inverted bowl, to prevent later collapse. A flue is left open in the center of the stacked wood. Clay is then packed around the wood and a hole made every three feet to admit restricted amounts of air.

Lighted charcoal is then placed in the flue and the flue covered. For three days, the wood smolders in this oxygen-depleted pile until the smoke emitting from the flue turns blue. Air is then completely excluded until the smoldering ceases. The charcoal is removed, stacked and transported to market.[14]

The son supported the family with this charcoal burning. Around Jo Daviess County, he was known as the "the Coal Boy." With money earned, John paid for the homestead land in April 1847 (before his father left for the gold rush) and eventually took title under his own name.

John was said to have had an especially good memory. Even before he was able to read, he memorized the Ten Commandments and won a prize at Sunday school. He began regular school at the age of seven, attending for three months during the winter, for a total of eight terms. Later, he sent his sister, Mary Lovisa ("Laura")[15], to the Galena Academy. By 1850, as his brothers grew older, John was able to attend high school in Galena for one term, boarding at the home of a Mr. Hallet. In January of 1852, after his father's return, he entered the Rock River Seminary in nearby Mt. Morris in Ogle County, Illinois, where he remained for four months; and, again the following year, for nine months.

While in residence, he made many friends among his fellow students, who would later distinguish themselves in public life. Among the subjects he studied were geometry, moral science, political economy and the Latin classics. He was a vigorous debater and a Democrat in his political convictions. While at school, he delivered an oration on the subject of patriotism, which won great praise. A popular member of the Amphictyonic Society, he orated regularly at the weekly meetings and was admitted to the Hekadelphoi Society, a private club of uncertain purpose.

Rawlins left the seminary in June 1853 and returned to charcoal burning. A few months later, the twenty-two year old was driving to market two yoke of oxen, laden with charcoal. The weather was uncommonly hot and the oxen soon tired at the foot of a hill, compelling Rawlins to halt and await the coolness of early morning. Next day, he drove his team to the Galena station of the Illinois Central Railroad, where his oxen again gave out. Some contractors took notice of his plight and bought his team, wagon and the load of charcoal for $250. With money in his pocket, he decided to give up charcoal burning and try his hand at the law. In those days, a son was bound to his parents until his twenty-first birthday, at which time he could leave home to seek his fortune.

After casting about, Rawlins found an opportunity in the law office of Isaac P. Stevens, Esq. of Galena.

He began work as a clerk, devoting his full time to the study of the law.[16] Within a year, he was admitted to the bar and taken into partnership by his employer. Ten months later the senior partner retired and relinquished the practice to his junior.

Galena, by this time, had grown into a cosmopolitan metropolis of 14,000 people and even boasted of a four-story, two-hundred room hotel.[17] Steamboats lined the wharfs, and rows of warehouses bustled with activity.

Rawlins was energetic and resourceful; and the law practice grew rapidly. He was especially successful with juries, which admired his simple and honest demeanor. The rugged young man received excellent advice early in his career when, as an assistant counsel to John M. Douglas, later president of the Illinois Central Railroad, he was encouraged to address the jury as if he was relating a series of facts to his mother.

He became a Freemason, a member of the Miners Lodge No. 273, and a good friend of the man who helped found the chapter, Ely S. Parker, about whom more will be said. A close bond was formed between Rawlins and the other Masons of Galena, which continued into his army service.

In 1856, Rawlins met the twenty-three year old Emily Smith from Goshen, New York, who was visiting her uncle, Bradner Smith, in Galena. She was the daughter of Hiram[18] Smith, a successful butcher in Goshen, and Sarah Bull Smith.[19] Goshen is an old New York town, the county seat of Orange County. Noah Webster, the father of the modern dictionary, taught in Goshen in the 1780's.

Emily Smith Rawlins, first wife of John A. Rawlins
Alfred Muller Collection, Steve Repp curator

John Rawlins was among the young men of Galena who showed the visitor great attention.[20] The two were married in Galena on June 5, 1856 and settled into a small cottage at 517 Hill Street, next door to a twin cottage belonging to William R. Rowley, his friend and fellow Mason. Rowley had been clerk of the county court and later, clerk of the circuit court. He was known for common sense, energy and tact.[21]

Three children were born to the couple: James, Jane Louisa ("Jennie") and Emily.[22] For a while, the family had a woman to help with the chores.[23] After the birth of the third child, Emily developed the symptoms of consumption (tuberculosis) and had to rely on the Rawlins family in Guilford, to help care for the two older children.[24]

The law practice continued to expand, and Rawlins took on a law clerk, David Sheean, his sister's brother-in-law. In March 1857, Rawlins was elected for a one year term as city attorney for Galena. The following year he entered into partnership with his former law clerk, who had since been admitted to the bar.[25] The partnership continued until Rawlins departed for the army.

Rawlins was an earnest pleader, who relied less on theatrics or technicalities than on an honest, reasoned analysis and an appeal to common law. He is known to have been polite to witnesses, no matter which side their testimonies favored, and especially respectful to his elders. Juries sensed that they had common roots with this dark haired, dark eyed, intense young man, and they delighted to see that he was no stranger to hard work. As time wore on, he became known as the best trial lawyer in Galena and the most popular man in the Congressional District.[26]

Evenings, he often met with three colleagues to discuss books, read poetry and argue politics. Rawlins was especially fond of Robert Burns and read aloud his poetry with a fine, resonant voice. Rawlins and two of his colleagues were Democrats; the fourth, an abolitionist.

Rawlins was a firm supporter of Stephen A. Douglas, senior Senator from Illinois and the sponsor of the Kansas-Nebraska Bill. This legislation allowed the settlers of the territory to determine for themselves the issue of slavery, and whether the territory would be admitted to the Union as a *free* or *slave* state. The Republicans, led by Abraham Lincoln, sought to exclude slavery from the western territories.

Prior to the second Lincoln-Douglas Debate in 1860, Douglas visited Galena, where he and Rawlins addressed an enthusiastic audience.[27]

One must not conclude that Rawlins or the other Douglas Democrats sought to encourage the spread of slavery. What popular sovereignty did, according to the Douglas Democrats, was to demonstrate to the South that the Northern states were not implacably hostile to Southern interests. Most Northern Democrats knew instinctively that slavery could never flourish in the Northern territories, with their crops of wheat and corn. A field tilled and harvested by free men spectacularly outperforms the slow and inefficient slave labor. There were the other considerations that made slavery non-competitive in the Northern territories, such as the cost of the slaves, their insurance, medical care, and the outlay for their non-productive years. In the 1860 Census for Kansas, only three slaves were recorded.

In the 1860 presidential election, Rawlins was nominated on the Democratic ticket for the office of Presidential Elector for the First Congressional District of Illinois. He challenged the Republican electoral candidate, Allen C. Fuller, also an eloquent speaker, to a series of debates. Meetings were held in each county of the Congressional district during September and October 1860 and were enthusiastically attended by the public.[28] Rawlins acquitted himself nobly and gained widespread respect as a fiery speaker.

Among the citizens who attended, was J. Russell Jones,[29] a shrewd co-owner of a large dry goods store, soon to be Lincoln's marshal for the Northern District of Illinois; and Elihu B. Washburne, a Republican Congressman. Washburne, a transplanted Yankee, had spent a year at the Cambridge (Massachusetts) Law School[30] before moving to Galena to practice law. Washburne ran for Congress in 1852 and was reelected to eight successive terms, evolving into a Republican Congressional leader and political confidant of Abraham Lincoln. He was described as "medium height, slight build, fair faced, well dressed with an air about him that indicated energy and pluck."[31] He was also a strict teetotaler.

Following the Republican victory in the election of November 1860, South Carolina, in a special convention, declared secession from the United States. Within forty days, six other Southern states followed.

While the nation was embroiled in meetings and demonstrations, Rawlins continued to practice law. The situation suddenly deteriorated when, on April 12, 1861, South Carolina secessionists fired on Fort Sumter in Charleston Harbor. The news stunned the Galena public. Stores closed their doors and businesses shut down, as crowds milled about the streets, seeking direction. On the evening of April

16th, a huge mass meeting was called at the county courthouse. One Democratic friend advised Rawlins not to attend; another cautioned him not to speak at the "Black Republican Meeting;" a third insisted that the federal government had no right to coerce the southern states. Many prominent citizens attended the meeting, among them Elihu B. Washburne, the Republican Congressman, who denounced the rebellious South and encouraged vigorous public support for the duly elected president of the United States.

Rawlins was called on to speak. Without hesitation, he mounted the platform and began a passionate address which went on for three-quarters of an hour. In a sonorous bass voice,[32] plainly heard throughout the vast gathering, Rawlins reviewed for his audience the origins of the dispute and the numerous efforts made to appease the South, such as the Compromise of 1850 and the Kansas-Nebraska Act. After denouncing the rebellious hot heads, he closed his speech with the words:

> I have been a Democrat all my life; but this is no longer a question of politics…Only one course is left for us. We will stand by the flag of our country and appeal to the God of Battle![33]

The speech was received with uproarious acclaim. Republicans cheered themselves hoarse, while the

Democrats, many of whom had been in doubt, were instantly won over.

Present in the courthouse was a forty year old former army officer, who had been uncertain as to what he should do. On the way home, he told a brother that he believed he ought to offer his services to the government.

The man was Ulysses S. Grant, son and employee of Jesse Grant, the owner of the leading leather store. Ulysses had graduated from the Military Academy at West Point, which at the time provided training in civil engineering. He had excelled in mathematics and the equestrian skills, but was otherwise an unremarkable cadet. Much of his spare time, was spent in zealously reading novels in the library, which may explain his striking literary style.[34] In his last year at the Academy, he served as a mere private in the cadet corps, a reflection of the low regard in which he was held by his superiors. He spent a few years in scattered posts, one of which was in St. Louis, where he chanced to meet the sister of his roommate at West Point, Julia Dent, who lived nearby on a 1,200 acre plantation with thirty slaves.[35] Julia was a quiet but strong willed woman, exceedingly athletic and a nimble horsewoman in her youth—almost a tomboy. Grant called her "the Boss." Years later, she astounded Grant by leaping fully dressed in fashionable attire over a fence, in response to a dare.

Grant graduated from the Military Academy in 1843. He would have preferred to leave the army and find employment as a mathematics instructor at a college, but he owed the army eight years of obligated service.

The Mexican War supervened in 1846, and Grant saw service as quartermaster (supplies) and commissary (food) officer for the Fourth Infantry Regiment. Among his duties was the transport of field equipment and supervision of a 2,000 mule train. He also found time to instruct General Tom Hammer, USV (U.S. Volunteers), in the duties of a brigadier general. Hammer was the congressman who had appointed Grant to the Military Academy and was now commander of a brigade of volunteer soldiers. As commissary officer, Grant contracted with the purveyors and at one time, set up and ran a bakery. He was given no combat command. He served in the Monterrey campaign under Zachary Taylor and in the Mexico City expedition with Winfield Scott. On several occasions, he left his command and participated in combat. On one critical occasion, he had a squad disassemble a pack howitzer and bring it up to a church belfry outside of the walls of Mexico City. When the cannon was put together, he fired on the Mexican troops and helped force an entry into the city. He was awarded two brevets for gallantry and service.[36] He also began drinking in Mexico.

After the war, Grant married Julia Dent. He served in Sacketts Harbor, a lonely post on Lake Ontario in New York. While there, his wife got him to take a temperance pledge and to join a temperance society. We may be sure that he was not just a casual drinker at the time. Thereafter, when posted to Detroit, Michigan, he reverted to heavy drinking, while his wife was back in St. Louis, having their first child. He served another short tour of duty in Sacketts Harbor.

His regiment was then ordered to the West Coast. Grant left by ship without his wife, who was again pregnant. During the journey over the Isthmus of Panama the regiment and its dependents travelled by the Panama Railroad for over half of the sixty mile journey, then by dugout canoe on the Chagres River to Cruces, twenty-five miles from Panama City on the Pacific. There, they found themselves stranded when the contractor failed to provide the mules necessary for the remaining journey to the coast. Disease promptly began to take its toll. Grant took charge and by paying the local alcalde twice the usual hire for the mules, acquired enough mounts to start up a mule train, but not before one-tenth of the soldiers and dependents had succumbed to cholera.[37]

Grant was made a company commander while stationed on the Pacific coast. He engaged in several business ventures (cattle, ice, potato farming, wood, and hostelry[38]) in an effort to raise money to send for his family, but the businesses were all unsuccessful. He began to drink heavily, and eventually his commanding officer felt obliged to ask for his resignation.

With all the opportunities beckoning in civilian life, army resignations were not uncommon. Thirty of his West Point schoolmates tendered their resignation from the army within the next seventeen months,[39] but not for heavy drinking or neglect of duty. His regimental commander must have been sorely provoked to have rid his unit of an officer with two brevets and commendable conduct on the Isthmus of Panama.

The rest is a familiar story. Grant left the army in 1854 and made his way to St. Louis.[40] At the time he had two children. He built a house for his family and began to farm, but even with four years of great effort, the farm failed. He failed at other businesses and in December 1859 was compelled to ask his father for assistance.

This must have devastated Jesse Grant. Jesse's father, Noah Grant, had served in the Revolutionary Army from Bunker Hill to Yorktown and ended up a drunkard, who squandered his possessions and cast out Jesse at an early age, to make his own way in the world.[41] Further, Jesse was disturbed by the fact that Julia owned two women slaves. In his youth, Jesse had lived at the home of John Brown's family, which left him a fierce abolitionist.

Jesse Grant had become a successful leather tanner and merchant. He owned a leather shop in Galena, for the wholesale and retail sale of tanned leather, saddlery, bits, tack and horse hardware. It was a large, four-story store fronting on two parallel streets, with a place in the cellar for sizing the skins.[42] The firm also bought hides in Galena and shipped them to Covington, Kentucky, for tanning.[43] The Galena store was run by his two sons, Simpson and Orville. Jesse Grant resided in Covington and visited the store a few weeks every year, but Simpson more or less ran the business.[44] "Jesse also owned three other leather stores in Ohio, Wisconsin and Iowa, and was thought to be worth $150,000.[45] He wore gold spectacles, owned a piano[46] and had a library of thirty-five books.[47]

Since Simpson was suffering from terminal consumption,[48] Jesse was anxious that his oldest son,

Ulysses, learn the trade. Ulysses was paid 600 dollars a year, later increased to 800 dollars, far more than the usual salary for a clerk; but from this, money had to be set aside to satisfy his outstanding creditors. Rent was $15 a month[49] for a cozy, two-story brick house with appropriate outbuildings. Simpson shared the house with Ulysses and his family.[50] At the outset, Julia employed no domestic help[51] (except for "Julie," her personal maid and ex-slave[52]) but soon had two women[53] to help care for the house and the four children.

Ulysses was the billing and collection agent for the firm. He purchased and handled hides, some of which weighed 250 pounds.[54] He also kept the books and somewhat reluctantly waited on customers.[55] Slowly, he began to learn the business, and, from all appearances, would soon become a principal.[56] In fact, he was well on the way to becoming a successful merchant and seemed to enjoy his work. Julia kept Grant from drinking, for the most part, no small task in Galena where most stores kept a barrel of whiskey for their customers. On one occasion Grant had gotten into difficulty in a tavern and was rescued by Ely Parker, who happened to be passing by. At least, that's the story the Parker family told.[57]

Parker was a powerful Seneca Indian, who handled himself well in a fight. He was born on the

Tonawanda Reservation in upstate New York, and after receiving a sound education, went on to study law. Upon completion of his law studies, he was denied admission to the bar, since, as an Indian, he was not a citizen of the United States. He sought work on the Erie Canal, quickly acquiring engineer's credentials. Later, the federal government sent him to Galena to supervise the construction of a customs house and a marine hospital. He and Grant were the only two in Galena to have engineering training.[58] Parker, a dedicated Freemason, helped found the first Masonic Lodge in Galena and became its Worshipful Master. John Rawlins was a member, as were Simpson and Orville Grant. Their father, Jesse, was also a Freemason.

    The twenty-nine year old Rawlins met the thirty-eight year old Grant in the leather store in the course of his legal work for J. R. Grant and Sons. Rawlins was an absolute teetotaler and made no effort to conceal his views. He told his friends that he would rather see them drink a glass of poison than a glass of whiskey.[59] In later years, Rawlins said that he did not think that Grant had taken especial notice of him.[60]

    Rawlins had heard about Grant even before Grant had come to Galena. Rawlins' next door neighbor was Mrs. Mary Lee, a half-sister to Grant's mother,

Hannah Grant, who was fond of relating Grant's adventures in the Mexican War. Rawlins listened attentively. As a youngster, Rawlins had regretted that he was too young to serve in the army, so on visits to the Grant store he questioned Grant closely about his wartime experiences. Grant's home was around the corner from Rawlins, no more distant than a five-minute walk. The Grant house was larger and more attractive than the Rawlins' cottage. Thanks to Jesse's generous salary, Grant was not meanly situated in Galena.

At the outbreak of hostilities Grant helped enroll a company of volunteers, then went to Springfield, carpetbag in hand, to assist the Governor in the adjutant general's office at a salary of two dollars a day.[61] With his quartermaster and commissary training, Grant was especially useful in the requisition of supplies.

Grant wrote the War Department, without success, to offer his services as an army officer. He tried to enlist the aid of General George McClellan in Cincinnati, also without success. Small wonder, since McClelland had seen him in Fort Vancouver, Oregon Territory, when Grant was drunk.[62] He then returned to Springfield to help train volunteers. Only when the regimental commander of the 21st Illinois Volunteers was found to be unfit for service, with no replacement immediately available, did the governor offer the regiment to Ulysses S. Grant. Twelve days later, when the time came for the regiment to reenlist for three year service, Grant received assistance from Congressman John A. McClernand, an old Black Hawk War soldier, and Congressman John Logan, a Mexican War veteran, both of whom encouraged the men with rousing enlistment talks. The 21st Illinois was Grant's first experience with volunteer soldiers.

Grant's regiment served in the Department of the West, with headquarters in St. Louis, one of sixty different departments, with ever changing names and boundaries. The Department of the West was first commanded by John C. Fremont, the explorer and later 1856 Republican presidential candidate. Fremont had earlier resigned from the army after a jurisdictional dispute in California. Now, as department commander, he lived under the constant threat that Missouri would fall to a rebel army, especially since his subordinate, Brigadier General Nathaniel Lyons, had suffered a disastrous defeat at Wilson's Creek in August 1861. Fremont had been criticized for withholding proper support.

Grant and the 21st Illinois spent a few months in northern Missouri and central Illinois without a significant encounter with the enemy. Fred, his eleven year old son, accompanied him for the first three weeks. Evidently, Julia Grant wanted a family presence beside him to forestall a relapse into drinking. In fact, she wanted the boy to remain longer, but Grant sent the boy home to Galena by upriver steamer. Grant prohibited the sale of whiskey in camp. At the time whiskey sold for twenty cents a gallon.[63]

A noted historian speculates that Grant's predisposition to alcohol may have been a factor in his success, since "he had nowhere to go but up, he could act with more boldness and decision than commanders who dared not risk failure."[64] Perhaps so, but it should be remembered that Grant was well-situated in Galena and had good prospects.

Rawlins, too, had been caught up in the war fervor. He helped his friends organize a cavalry regiment, and later, the 45th Illinois Infantry ("Lead Mine Regiment").

Meanwhile, his wife was in the terminal stages of consumption. At the time, not much was known about the disease. Louis Pasteur had yet to announce his germ theory (c. 1865) and Robert Koch, his description of the Tubercle Bacillus (1882). Emily and their children had gone home to Goshen, New York, to spend her last days with her family. Her condition worsened, and Rawlins traveled to Goshen to be with her in her final days.

While in Goshen, he saw an official notice in the New York *Tribune* that Ulysses S. Grant had been made a brigadier general. Lincoln had allotted four brigadier generalships to Illinois, and, thanks to Congressman Washburne, one had gone to Grant. The father, Jesse Grant, was, after all, a dedicated Republican[65] and J. R. Grant and Sons, a prominent business. More important, the commission was retroactive to May 17, 1861,[66] a month before even his colonel's commission, but the Senate did not confirm it until August 9th. Each brigadier general was allowed an assistant adjutant general, a quartermaster, commissary officer, and two aides-de-camp, selected from his command.

   General Grant sent a letter to Rawlins, formally offering him the position of assistant adjutant general (AAG). "I am entitled to a captain and acting adjutant general. I guess you had better come and take it."[67] Grant's letter to Rawlins was sent to Galena and forwarded to Goshen. Grant wrote Julia to ask Orville to urge Rawlins to accept the offer.[68] Rawlins accepted the appointment on September 1st, two days after the death of his wife.[69] Following the funeral, he returned to Galena, but left the children in the Smith household in Goshen to be cared for by Emily's unmarried younger sister, Sarah.

Washburne was heartily in favor of the Rawlins appointment. Evidently Washburne, a strict alcohol abstainer, believed that if anyone could keep Grant sober, it would be Rawlins. However, since Rawlins was not immediately available because of his wife's illness, he feared that Grant might withdraw the offer. Grant reassured him:

> In regard to the appointment of Mr. Rawlins, I never had an idea of withdrawing it so long as he felt disposed to accept, no matter how long his absence. Mr. Rawlins was the first one I decided upon for a place with me and very much regret that family application has kept him away so long.[70]

In one of his letters, Grant misspelled Rawlins' name as "Rollins," which was the name recorded in the census of 1850 and 1860.

WAR IN THE WEST

Grant assumed command on September 4, 1861 of the District of Southeast Missouri,[71] with headquarters at Cairo, Illinois. His district was a subordinate part of the Department of the West (later Department of the Missouri). Cairo lay at the junction of the Mississippi and Ohio Rivers, buried in mud and overrun with rats and mosquitoes. A journalist described Cairo:

> ...rain, mud, hogs nosing piles along the sidewalk; tinkling pianos in the bawdy houses along front Street; great lobby of St. Charles Hotel, where captains rubbed elbows with cotton speculators, gamblers and travelers; acres of riverboats tied up along the levee; the smell of the warehouses,...whiskey-pungent air of waterfront taverns.[72]

Grant arrived in Cairo wearing civilian clothing. His somewhat ornate uniform, then on order, would follow shortly. While a regimental commander, he had had his second-in-command officiate at dress parades.[73]

In addition to his district, Grant had been given overall command of the naval gunboats in the region, soon to be commanded by Navy Captain Andrew H. Foote. Grant outranked the other brigadier generals in his district, by virtue of the early date of his commission and the fact that he had once held a commission in the regular army.

Forty and fifty miles up the Ohio River were the towns of Paducah and Smithland at the mouths of the Tennessee and Cumberland Rivers, respectively. Both rivers had enormous strategic importance, which was immediately apparent to Grant. The Tennessee River flows 650 miles through Alabama, Tennessee and Kentucky, before entering the Ohio River. The Cumberland River courses about the same distance through Tennessee and Kentucky. Both were navigable for hundreds of miles upriver.

The day after Grant arrived in Cairo, he received word that the rebels were occupying Columbus, Kentucky, a strategic port on the Mississippi River only twenty miles from Cairo. Any enemy activity in Kentucky was of enormous concern. "I hope I have God on my side," wrote Lincoln, "but I *must* have Kentucky!" Kentucky was divided in its loyalties, but chiefly favored the Union cause. It provided 90,000 enlistments for the Union; 25-40,000 for the Confederacy.[74] At the time, Kentucky was still struggling to remain out of the conflict, but the capture and fortification of Columbus by the Confederate General (Bishop) Leonidas Polk had upset the "neutrality" and provided Grant with justification to occupy Paducah, even without Fremont's direct authorization.

Grant boldly embarked two regiments and a battery of artillery on two gun boats and on September 6, 1861 occupied Paducah, Kentucky, at the mouth of the Tennessee River without a shot being fired. Brigadier General C. F. Smith, his former Commandant of Cadets at West Point, later arrived with additional troops for Paducah and Smithland.

Rawlins reported to headquarters at Cairo on September 14th and took up his duties. Headquarters was then on the first floor of Safford's Bank.[75] Rawlins found Grant seated behind the cashier's window hole, with a waste paper basket under him, sorting letters, requisitions and papers.[76] Army funds were kept in the bank vault on the first floor.[77] Before Rawlins' arrival, Grant had been performing the adjutant's work, staying up until midnight.[78] "General Grant's office was substantially in his hat or in his pockets," someone observed, and "half his general orders were blowing about the sand and dirt of the streets of Cairo."[79] Considering the lack of clerical help, Rawlins was amazed at Grant's promptness in replying to letters.

After Rawlins had arrived, Grant moved his office upstairs to a front room. An orderly was selected to serve as clerk. Rawlins soon established the headquarters protocol, while "General Grant sat, smoking his Meerschaum pipe[80] with curved stem, at one of the windows gazing at the flotilla of gun-boats and the Kentucky shore beyond."[81]

The first order of business for the new adjutant was to obtain from Grant a solemn promise in writing that he would abstain from alcohol. Rawlins was displeased with the roistering and drinking by the staff officers, who exposed Grant to the temptation of alcohol.[82] Among the heavy drinkers were Captain Clark B. Lagow and William S. Hillyer, both aides-de-camp, who had been with Grant since the 21st Illinois service. Hillyer had befriended Grant during his year in St. Louis, when Grant was a rent collector Aside from his drinking habits, Hillyer was a loyal advisor, and his wife, a close friend and often a companion to Julia Grant. Both Hillyer and Lagow were "good old boys, partial to good food, strong drink and poker."[83] Nor were they the only "hail fellows" on the staff.

Rawlins got Grant to prohibit alcohol at headquarters. The surgeon, Dr. John Brinton, was ordered not to dispense alcohol to the staff, except for urgent medical reasons.[84] Anyone who offered a drink to Grant faced demotion and exile (if caught). The staff objected, but Rawlins prevailed; or so he thought. Staff officers who drank in their tents were sent back to line regiments. Cadwallader saw the matter differently:

> If one of the staff had in some way come into the possession of a bottle or demijohn of whiskey and wished to share it with a caller or a friend, he took him into his tent, closed the flap and drank with the utmost secrecy.[85]

Some of the officers of high rank objected to the lowly captain's strictures, but Grant supported Rawlins.[86] Despite Rawlins' best intentions, one cannot be sure that his efforts significantly curtailed the quantity of spirits consumed by the staff. In those days, the annual male consumption of spirits in the United States was five gallons.

Rawlins took over the job of the returns, reports, correspondence and orders. Wrote one adjutant:

> An adjutant should be a man well posted in alarms of the service, know the right flank from the left and the front from the rear. He should be able to tell, without hesitation, a jackass battery from one of one-hundred pounder Parrotts; should be able to ride a horse without falling off, and to handle his saber and revolver without wounding himself or killing his

horse. He should know how to write the name of his commanding general and his own; the larger letters the better. He should be an adept in military correspondence and be able with Chesterfieldian courtesy to apply the cold steel of official rebuke to subordinate commanders.[87]

How long it took Rawlins to satisfy these requirements is unknown, but he was a fast learner.

Washburne paid a visit to Cairo in October 1861. He had invested political capital in Jesse Grant's son and needed to personally satisfy himself that all was well.[88] Some said that he had Grant on the brain.

On November 1st, Grant received a series of orders from Fremont, Commander of the Western Department, directing him to make a demonstration,[89] in order to discourage the Confederate commander, General Polk, from sending troops from Kentucky into Missouri. A demonstration is a show of force—a threat, rather than an engagement.

This was Fremont's last order to Grant. Earlier, he had issued an unsanctioned proclamation authorizing the death penalty for rebels found to possess firearms and directed that their slaves be emancipated. When ordered by Lincoln to withdraw the proclamation, he refused. Lincoln replaced him on November 19th with Major General Henry W. Halleck.

Grant set out on transports from Cairo on November 6th, with 3,500 men. General Charles F.

Smith, stationed in Paducah, was directed to make a simultaneous demonstration against Columbus. Grant later stated in his memoirs that, while in transit, he decided not to demonstrate but to attack, fearing his men were becoming unruly from their prolonged inactivity.[90] One finds this difficult to believe. Why would he embark 3,000 men to make a demonstration, when it could be accomplished by sending a few gunboats to shell Columbus?[91]

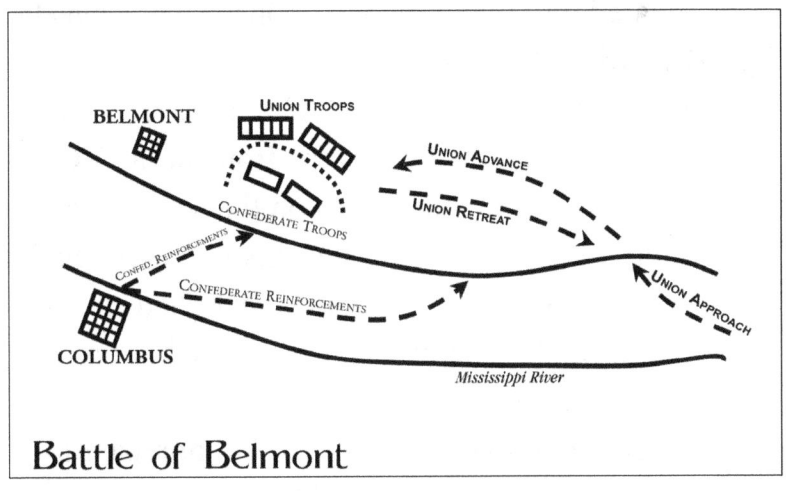

Battle of Belmont

Two day's rations had been issued to the men. Their destination was Belmont, Missouri, on the west bank of the Mississippi River, across the river from Columbus. After occupying Columbus on September 5th, Polk had turned it into a bristling defensive work with 142 heavy guns, to dominate traffic on the Mississippi River. Belmont was the obvious landing point for any proposed Confederate troop movement into Missouri. It had earlier been occupied by Federal troops, but Grant had ordered them withdrawn when they were threatened by a rebel gunboat. Grant speculated that if Belmont were occupied and Columbus threatened, the enemy might withdraw from Columbus.[92]

The following day steam transports carried the Union troops to two miles below the Belmont landing and disembarked the five regiments, which Grant had consolidated into two brigades.[93] One brigade was led by Brigadier General John A. McClernand, an ambitious and somewhat charismatic Illinois politician and friend of Lincoln. Both he and Grant had received their commissions on the same date, but Grant outranked him by virtue of his previous regular army commission. The brigades marched for two miles towards the enemy position, over bottom land covered with cornfields and timber.

The rebel commander was caught unprepared and barely had time to form his regiment into a defensive line. Despite their disjointed approach through broken terrain, the Union brigades penetrated the abatis enclosing the Confederate camp and after a brisk three hour battle, pushed the rebels to the river. Rawlins rode beside Grant during the battle. The loss of a horse in battle was considered by many as a measure of gallantry. Grant lost his horse when a bullet struck its stifle joint. He borrowed Hillyer's horse but in the melee, lost his own saddle and bridle.[94] McClernand lost three horses (one horse shot while being ridden, and two shot while being held). Instead of rounding up the enemy troops, the Union soldiers scattered through the enemy camp and began to loot and scavenge.

Meanwhile, Polk, in Columbus, quickly dispatched four regiments across the Mississippi to Belmont; two, to join up with the Confederate troops reforming near the embankment, and the others to take Grant's army in flank. Grant saw the approaching vessels and immediately recognized the danger. To draw the attention of his unruly hoard, he ordered Rawlins to have the enemy tents set on fire, which the staff proceeded to do. Panic swept the Union troops, but their officers managed to reform them. Grant led the soldiers back to their embankment, overcoming along the way brisk opposition from the newly arrived enemy regiments. Rawlins and Grant's servant, Bill Barnes, were among the last to board,[95] followed by Grant, riding his horse over a narrow gangway.[96]

Most of the 600 Union casualties were sustained during the retreat[97]—nineteen percent of the troops engaged—in this so-called minor effort. Many wounded were left behind, a measure of the desperation during the Union withdrawal. Later, some of the Union wounded were retrieved in a prisoner exchange. Grant lost his bay pony, saddle and the tack, altogether worth $250.[98] In the official report, he classified the encounter as a "raid." Had he called it a "battle," the outcome would have been a "repulse."[99] His report was dated Nov. 17, 1861, but, in fact, Grant wrote the revised Official Record in 1864, restating the purpose of the attack.[100]

McClernand, meanwhile, lost no time in sending his own battle report to his friend, President Lincoln, and received from him warm congratulations. When Rawlins learned of McClernand's action, he cursed:

> The bastard! The damned, stinking Judas bastard![101]

Despite McClernand's breech of military etiquette, Rawlins continued to maintain good relations with him.

After Belmont, Julia and the four children came to visit Grant, accompanied by the congenial Mrs. Hillyer.[102] Julia and the children moved into the apartments on the second floor of the bank and then to a house which reminded Julia of a barracks.[103] She frowned on Grant's ornate uniform, which Grant promptly replaced with field dress. Also, she made him trim his beard, which had been "long and shaggy."[104] A journalist observed:

> Everything seemed absolutely safer when she was present. Her quiet firm control of her husband seemed marvelous to those who had so often tried and failed.[105]

Grant devoted considerable time to administrative affairs. He oversaw the construction of winter quarters for the troops and procured supplies and equipment, travelling to as far as St. Louis and Springfield, Illinois, to collect the necessary stores.

Close attention was given to the purchase of steamboats and to the construction of seven gunboats and transports at the shipyard in Mound City, a few miles from Cairo. Each of the 150-foot gunboats would mount thirteen cannon, either thirty-two or sixty-four pounders. Fremont was the first to foresee the need for an inland navy to halt enemy traffic and had requested the services of a senior naval officer. In order to hasten construction of the seven gunboats, Grant offered liberal inducements to the builders. Since he usually lacked money to pay for supplies, he had to rely on government credit.

Grant insisted on full weight and quality for the stores and provisions delivered. His previous training as quartermaster and commissary officer was of invaluable help. Nevertheless, it was soon discovered that his quartermaster and his clerks had taken kickbacks and rigged the bidding. An article appeared in the *Chicago Tribune* alleging egregious fraud in the quartermaster department. Stanton sent an assistant secretary of war, Thomas A. Scott, to Cairo to investigate. He reported that conditions were "as bad as could be imagined…A regular system of fraud appears to have been adapted."[106] A court martial was ordered, but the guilty parties escaped punishment because of their political connections.

Rawlins, too, was skillful in detecting scams and corruption. "No rogue ever got a chance to make an indecent proposal."[107] Contractors protested. Some invented stories about Grant's drunkenness, embroidering on the gossip attending Grant's resignation from the army. A good friend of Lincoln tried to intervene on behalf of the contractors, but Grant banished him from the district. Another investigator was sent to examine the contracts with the shipbuilders. He was an honest man, but crack-handed in his investigations of shipbuilding activities. Hillyer was especially helpful in dealing with this nuisance.[108] When an exasperated Grant had the newcomer arrested, the inspector charged that Grant had been "beastly drunk" and that he "staggered drunk in public."[109]

Anxious to advance his own interests, General McClernand gave clandestine support to the drinking charges and sent the investigator back to Washington to report that on March 13th, Grant had been "gloriously drunk."[110] Twenty officers signed a statement depicting a wild debauch on that date, the details of which challenge credulity.[111]

Alarmed at these and other reports, Representative Washburne wrote Rawlins, inquiring about the drinking problem. Rawlins replied on December 30, 1861 in a somewhat rambling, three double-page letter that the charges of drunkenness were untrue. Grant had taken an occasional glass with a visiting dignitary but "…no man can say that at any time since I have been with him has he drunk liquor enough to in the slightest unfit him for business." Grant had promised that "he should not during the continuance of the war again taste liquor of any kind." For verification, Rawlins referred Washburne to six men who had been closely associated with Grant, among them Captain (later Flag Officer) Foote, who was an absolute abstainer. He concluded:

> I pledge you my word for it, should General Grant at any time become an intemperate man or a habitual drunkard, I will notify you immediately and will ask to be removed from duty on his staff…[112]

Rawlins first showed the letter to Grant, who told him to send it. Washburne was familiar with Rawlins' reputation for probity. He accepted his word and calmed Grant's critics in Washington. Rawlins was adamant about prohibiting liquor at headquarters. When one regular army officer arrived with a large keg of whiskey in his possession, Rawlins had the bung removed, and the keg thrown into the river.[113] It would be naïve to think that this dried up the supply of alcohol at headquarters.

Henry Halleck, meanwhile, had replaced Fremont in what was now called "The Department of the Missouri." A West Point graduate, he served in the Mexican War, not as a line commander but as an engineer (as had Robert E. Lee and George McClellan). He resigned from the army to enter business and to practice law and was successful in both pursuits. In addition to writing two law books, he was a military scholar, fond of displaying his knowledge of bygone battles. Somewhat critical and brusque, he showed excessive regard for his own reputation. Rawlins once remarked that if he had to endure Halleck's scorn, he would resign.[114]

Grant had visited Halleck's headquarters in St. Louis in January 1862 and had tried to interest him, without success, in a campaign to capture Forts Henry and Donelson.[115] Flag Officer Foote was also supportive of the plan. Fort Henry was situated on the Tennessee River and Fort Donelson on the Cumberland, both guarding against Union advances upriver. Meanwhile, when Lincoln issued a preemptory Order No. 1 on January 27, 1862 calling for a general advance in all active departments, Halleck promptly agreed to an attack—but only on Fort Henry.[116]

Before the expedition was underway, Rawlins carefully studied the troop and supply requirements and made thorough provision for reinforcements.[117] Brigadier General William T. Sherman was ordered to Paducah to replace Smith and to keep Grant's army supplied with men and supplies.

Sherman was a West Point graduate who resigned from the army after eleven years of service. He had several unsuccessful business ventures before becoming superintendant of a Louisiana military college. Reentering army service at the onset of hostilities, he is said to have panicked during his first command and failed to destroy an important railroad bridge, vital to the enemy. Halleck and Grant were willing to give him an opportunity to redeem himself.

Rawlins strove to maintain friendly relations with the press. He used the newspapermen to circulate exaggerated reports of the Union strength in Cairo. Later, he turned over the censorship responsibility to a volunteer aide, Colonel John Riggin, Jr., who allowed an article to slip by, which described a pending river expedition. Fortunate for Grant, by the time the new commander in St. Louis read the account in the newspapers, the campaign was underway.[118]

On February 1, 1862 Lieutenant Colonel James B. McPherson reported for duty as staff engineer, the same position he had held on Halleck's staff. McPherson had been an outstanding student at West Point, and his expertise in military matters was of enormous help to Grant's staff. Rawlins was quick to appreciate the talents of this most competent officer, and they became close friends. The fact that McPherson was a strict abstainer only improved his relations with Rawlins. Before undertaking his new mission, Grant sent Julia and the family to Jesse Grant's home in Covington, Kentucky.[119]

The next day, Grant set out for Fort Henry, fifty miles up the Tennessee River, just over the Kentucky border. Loaded on the seven gunboats and nine transports were 17,000 Union troops. Sherman in Paducah was expected to send reinforcements.

The Surgeon John Brinton relates a humorous incident while en route. Rawlins had a magnificent bay horse with a luxurious tail with long hair, which almost reached the floor, a gift from a Galena friend. One morning the hair was gone. Rawlins "was dumb with wrath"[120] and vowed to shoot the man who was responsible.

Grant roared with laughter, knowing that the hair had been chewed off by a mule. Thereafter, whenever Rawlins rode in advance, the sight of the hairless tail would stir mirth.[121]

Reconnaissance had shown that construction on Fort Henry was still unfinished. Within four days, the fort was captured, chiefly through the efforts of the gunboat cannonades; but the 2,000 men in the enemy garrison managed to escape to nearby Fort Donelson.

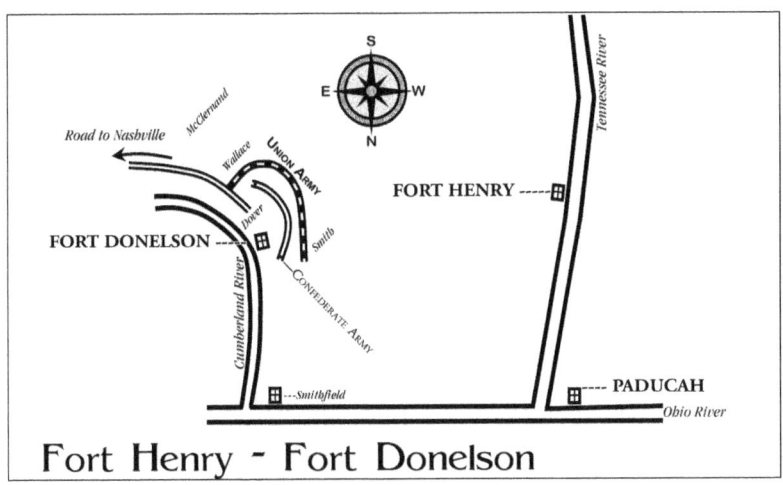

Fort Henry - Fort Donelson

Grant disembarked his troops and organized them into three brigades. The navy flotilla backed down the Tennessee River to the Ohio, then went up the Cumberland River to Fort Donelson.

The weather was warm when the troops started out for Fort Donelson, twelve miles away. Characteristically, Grant had little idea of the difficulties that lay ahead.[122] His men lacked tents, stores and provisions which were later supplied by boats coming up the Cumberland River from Paducah. Rawlins observed that:

> Grant was always ready whenever he had what he thought a sufficient number of men without regard to the number of days they had arms in their hands to give battle.[123]

On February 12th, Grant marched his men to Fort Donelson, and promptly invested the fort. No more than a collection of a few buildings, the fort was situated on a hill overlooking the Cumberland and protected by three miles of hastily-dug entrenchments. Heavy cannon emplacements traversed the river.

During the first night, a rebel deserter brought information that enemy reinforcements were on the way to Fort Donelson and would attack the Union line the next day. Rawlins doubted the story and responded in kind. He ordered the prisoner held within earshot, then read aloud a spurious dispatch which stated that Sherman had captured Columbus. Later, the guard was instructed to let the captive escape, but to fire a few harmless shots to send him on his way. The prisoner "escaped" back to Fort Donelson.[124]

Snow fell the first night. The wind blew from the west, and the temperature dropped to ten below zero.

The soldiers on both sides lacked winter clothing and tents. Some froze to death. The next day the 10,000 reinforcements sent by Sherman (from Buell's army) arrived, so that Grant at least had parity in number with the enemy. Nevertheless, a besieging force usually requires at least three times the strength of an entrenched enemy. Union headquarters had been set up in a small farmhouse nearby.

On February 15th, the enemy launched a sudden attack which mauled Grant's right wing (McClernand). Unaccountably, they did not press their attack, although they had inflicted considerable damage. During the early battle, Grant had been absent from his command post, having left at five a.m. to consult with the wounded naval commander aboard a gunboat. When he returned eight hours later (!), Rawlins quickly apprised him of the perilous situation. They saw an officer running from the battlefield. "We're cut to pieces!" screamed the deserter. Rawlins drew out his revolver, but Grant restrained him.[125]

Grant quickly surmised that the purpose of the enemy attack on the Union right wing (McClernand) was to clear the way for an enemy escape to Nashville,[126] since the right wing blocked the road. Consequently, he reasoned, the enemy must have weakened its line somewhere, to bolster its attack on

McClernand's brigade. Grant ordered C. F. Smith's brigade, commanding the Union left wing, to attack the opposing enemy line, and he sent whatever reserves he had to McClernand, who quickly regained lost ground. With escape cut off, the enemy surrendered the next day. It is also possible that Grant ordered the counter-attack without the close reasoning ascribed to him and that Smith's brigade, alone, was able to respond.

The capture of both forts had great strategic importance which the public was quick to recognize. A portrait of a general with a long beard, purporting to be that of Grant, appeared on the cover of *Harper's Weekly*.[127] Not only did Grant free up two important rivers, but he had captured a whole enemy army—*fifteen thousand men!* Especially striking was Grant's "unconditional surrender" reply to the enemy general, when asked about terms.

The Donelson campaign gave Rawlins an important insight into military tactics. By now, the weakness in staff organization had become apparent. Grant personally had attended to the transportation details, a task usually allocated to the staff.[128] He even insisted on dictating such orders as the placement of pickets, infractions of discipline, assistance for the Union refugees and a myriad of other matters;[129] but such attention to detail was characteristic of Grant and would continue throughout the war.

Nevertheless, a more specific assignment of duties was needed. This was contained in General Orders #21:

> Captain Rawlins AAG, assisted by Captain Rowley AAG, to keep the records, consolidate returns and forward all documents to their proper destination; Captain Hillyer, Aide-de-Camp (ADC), to collect the returns from the subordinate commands; Captain Lagow ADC and Colonel John Riggin, Jr., ADC to supervise passes, supplies, coal, forage, etc; Colonel Webster,[130] Chief of Staff and artillery officer, to advise Grant and give proper attention to miscellaneous matters; Captain Hawkins inspecting quartermaster and commissary and Lt. Col. J. B. McPherson, Chief Engineer.[131]

William R. Rowley was the Rawlins' next door neighbor in Galena. He joined the army after Donelson. T. S. Bowers, AAG, a former newspaperman, was serving in the ranks before Grant commissioned him and gave him a staff appointment. John Riggin, Jr., from St. Louis, had joined the staff in Cairo. He had entered military service as a private and quickly rose up through the ranks.

Following the capture of the twin forts, Grant and Rawlins left for Nashville, to consult with General Buell, commander of the Department of the Ohio, who had not yet entered the city. Buell was a regular army officer with twenty-three years of service,[132] who had a prickly dislike for any intrusion into his jurisdiction. Grant and Rawlins toured Nashville unguarded and visited the widow of President Polk.[133] Grant had known her late husband in the Mexican campaign.

Once Grant had left Fort Donelson, his daily reports to Halleck ceased. Later, it was learned that although reports had been written, a Confederate sympathizer in the telegraph office failed to forward them. Halleck was incensed at the omission, as well as by the fact that Grant had left Donelson without permission. To add to Halleck's ire, the Northern newspapers had reported appalling conditions among the Union troops stationed at Fort Donelson, due to lack of adequate supplies.[134] Scurvy and smallpox had broken out, and, short of provisions, some troops were plundering the countryside.

Old charges against Grant were promptly revived. On March 4th Halleck wrote to George McClellan in Washington:

> A rumor has just reached me that since the taking of Fort Donelson, General Grant has resumed his former bad habits.[135]

Rawlins was furious when he learned of the accusations. He quickly let it be known that:

I was near him [Grant] all the time. We were seldom an hour apart. He was never drunk. He did not drink to excess.[136]

Halleck suspended Grant and ordered him to return to Fort Donelson. Rawlins immediately wrote to Congressman Washburne and urged that the suspension be lifted. Even McClernand endorsed the appeal. Soon, investigation confirmed that Grant had been submitting reports and that his presence in Nashville had a reasonable purpose. The controversy demonstrated to Rawlins and others that Grant would never be given the benefit of a doubt.

In the wake of the capture of Fort Donelson, the enemy was compelled to evacuate Columbus, and Western Tennessee fell into Union hands. Both Grant and McClernand were made major generals USV (Volunteers). Rawlins was promoted to major, USV on April 14, 1862.

One of Grant's generals, Charles F. Smith, the reliable and effective brigade commander at Fort Donelson, had also become the target of drinking charges. Grant, who revered and respected Smith, his former West Point instructor, forbade any unfavorable criticism of Smith to leave his headquarters. Rawlins himself took on the job of sifting through the newsmen's dispatches. Censorship was not a regular practice at Grant's headquarters, unless a dispatch conveyed information intended to benefit the enemy. Within a few weeks, General C. F. Smith died from a leg infection, and the close censorship ended.

With Julia Grant gone to Covington, Kentucky for a visit with Jesse and Hannah Grant,[137] the responsibility for safeguarding Grant reverted to Rawlins. In fairness to Grant, Wilson writes:

> It has never been charged that it [drinking] at any time induced him [Grant] to march or fight when he ought not to have done so, nor to refrain from marching or fighting when circumstances were favorable to the cause…On the other hand it is not to be denied that it materially increased the influence and responsibility of Rawlins at headquarters or that it led to a sort of moral supervision over Grant…which, although self imposed by Rawlins, was of the greatest advantage both to Grant and to the country. This fact…was generally known to the leading officers of the army at the time and did much to secure not only their support and respect for Rawlins but their loyal cooperation in all measures of discipline, as well as in all of the great movements which were concluded by Grant.[138]

It helped that Rawlins was well liked and respected by the staff officers, even the drinkers, and especially by the Democrat generals in the volunteer army.

Following the capture of the twin forts, Halleck was given superseding authority over both the Army of the Ohio (Buell) and the Army of the Tennessee (Grant); and Grant was given back his command. Halleck ordered Grant and his 40,000 troops to proceed by riverboat to a little steamboat landing called Pittsburg Landing on the west bank of the Tennessee River, twenty miles from Corinth, Mississippi. Here, General Don Carlos Buell and his 50,000 men, marching from Nashville, would link up with him. Together, they would bring overwhelming force against Corinth, an important Confederate rail center, with tracks leading to Mobile, Memphis, Chattanooga and Charleston.

Grant's immediate concern was not with the strategic importance of Corinth but with the enemy occupying the city. He was a dogged commander, with unshakable confidence that his will and his determination would prevail in battle. "Find out where your enemy is," he wrote.

> Get at him as soon as you can. Strike at him as hard as you can and as often as you can and keep moving on.

As to strategy:

> I don't believe in strategy, in the popular understanding of the term. I believe in getting up just as close to the enemy and with as little loss of life as possible.[139]

All his military values, the good and the bad, would be sorely tested in the battle that lay ahead.

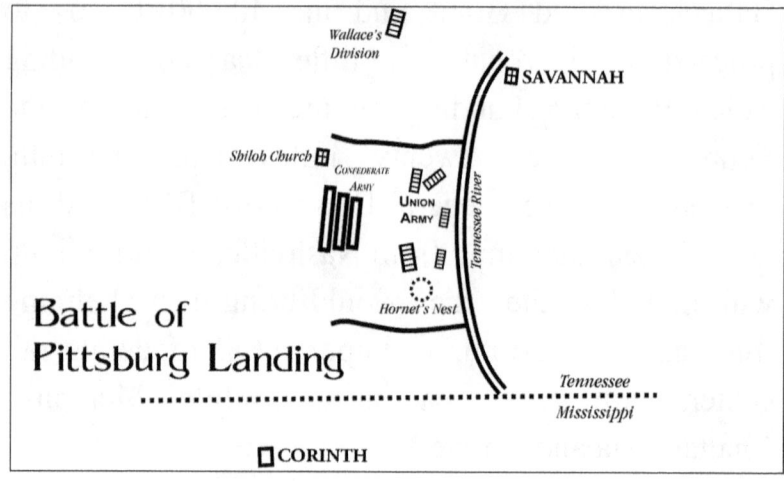

Grant had encamped his five divisions of the Army of the Tennessee for nearly a month at Pittsburg Landing, with Sherman left in command.[140] A steep bluff rose above the landing. Three miles from the landing was a little Methodist Church called "Shiloh," that gave the ensuing battle its name.[141] Another Union division under General Lew Wallace was camped five miles away.

The renowned Confederate general, Albert Sidney Johnston, a Texan and former regular army officer, planned to attack Grant's army before Buell could link up with him. Buell, in turn, was in no hurry to join Grant. It took him twenty-two days to move his Army of the Ohio a distance of 140 miles from Nashville.

Grant, Rawlins and staff arrived on March 16th, a week after his army had first encamped. He set up his headquarters at Savannah, Tennessee, on the east bank of the Tennessee River, some twelve miles downriver from Pittsburg Landing. Here, he and his staff would remain for three weeks, awaiting Buell. Halleck, himself, had specifically selected Savannah as a site for the rendezvous, peering at a map.

Since the roads were muddy, there was little concern that the enemy could approach Pittsburg Landing undetected. Enemy reinforcements were known to be arriving daily in Corinth. Reports had been received that thirteen trains had reached Corinth, each with twenty cars loaded with rebel troops. This added an additional 10,000 men to the rebel roster and brought the total to 40,000.[142] Grant estimated enemy strength at twice that number.

No entrenchments or fortifications had been ordered for the Union camp. Grant had McPherson, the engineer, lay out a defensive line, which could be easily fortified, but issued no orders for entrenchments.[143] Grant later stated that he preferred to train his raw troops, rather than to have them dig defenses. Perhaps, but basic entrenchments could have been dug in four hours, and Grant had had three weeks to prepare. In a word, Grant (and Sherman) had failed to exercise proper caution.

The enemy marched unobserved from Corinth for three days in inclement weather over broken terrain. On Sunday April 6, 1862 at six a.m., three waves of enemy soldiers attacked the 35,000 Union troops.

When they heard the distant sound of gunfire, Grant and Rawlins rushed by steamboat to the battlefield, cancelling a meeting with Buell, who had arrived the night before in advance of his troops.[144] Grant reached the landing at eight a.m.[145] McPherson was already on hand, defining for each division commander his perimeter. Fighting was furious on a three-mile battle line. Five Union divisions struggled to form up, to withstand the Confederate onslaught. Grant was everywhere, with Rawlins and McPherson beside him, encouraging his commanders; organizing the flow of ammunition; reforming the crowds of skulkers cowering at the landing. Again and again, he showed himself in the thick of battle, often at the peril of his life.

Pressing messages were sent to Buell's army (via Hillyer), and to Lew Wallace (via Rowley), whose 5,000 man division was encamped only five miles away. Rawlins restored order at the landing. He barred one boat from docking, fearful that the skulkers would attempt to board it. Another vessel arrived with several badly needed ammunition barges in tow. When a shell exploded nearby, the captain tried to slip the moorings, but Rawlins stopped him from pulling away by threatening to shoot him.[146]

By 2:30 pm Lew Wallace and his division still had not arrived, so Grant sent Rawlins and McPherson to hurry them along.[147] When they caught up with Wallace, Rawlins urged him to abandon his artillery, to speed up the march, but Wallace refused. Rawlins was prepared to arrest him, but McPherson thought it futile to do so.[148] So Wallace marched and countermarched for seven hours over fifteen miles of terrain.[149] The first of Buell's army reached Pittsburg Landing in late afternoon, but Wallace and his troops did not arrive until 7:15 p.m., despite the frantic efforts of Rawlins and McPherson. Wallace spent the rest of his life offering excuses. "I was the victim of a mistake," Wallace later wrote.[150]

To the left of the Union position stood a sunken road later called "the hornet's nest". Here, a Union division had withstood a dozen attempts to outflank Grant's left wing, before being enveloped and captured. By nightfall, both armies were exhausted. The Union Army had been pushed to the riverbank and compressed into a shrunken perimeter near the landing.

Fortunate for the Union Army, the Confederate commander had been killed during the battle, and his successor lacked the reserves to press the attack. At nightfall, the Union gunboats harassed the enemy as did the artillery of Colonel Webster, firing from the heights above the landing.[151] The arrival of Buell's fresh troops,[152] and the belated appearance of Wallace's division decided the outcome.

The following day, the enemy was repulsed and the Confederate troops, short of ammunition, were driven back to Corinth. Grant later wrote that he had never despaired of victory:

> There comes a time in every hard-fought battle, when both armies are nearly or quite exhausted... whichever after first renews the fight is sure to win.[153]

This is a lofty assessment from a badly mauled general, who was saved by the providential arrival of fresh troops from another command. Neither Grant nor Buell chose to pursue the retreating enemy army.

The immediate response in the North to news of the battle was jubilation and praise for Grant. Soon rumors surfaced about his unpreparedness, his early absence from the battlefield and the familiar, but untrue, charges of drunkenness. The losses had been appalling. The Union suffered 13,000 casualties, the enemy 11,000. The total losses to both armies at Pittsburg Landing (24,000) exceeded even those at Antietam (22,000).[154]

Halleck rushed to Pittsburg Landing and took command of the two armies. Grant was given a meaningless appointment and his troops were assigned to General George Thomas, a solemn regular army man from Virginia, with twenty-four years of army service.[155] He had been a division commander in Buell's Army.

Halleck was irate. Before the battle, he had specifically instructed Grant to ensure that his camp was properly fortified. To prove his point, Halleck, himself, marched the combined armies of Thomas and Buell toward Corinth, creeping along the twenty miles and fortifying every campground along the way. After four weeks of exaggerated caution, the 120,000-man army arrived at Corinth to find the city deserted. Still, Halleck could insist that had the army moved faster, it would have had to fight for the city. To this Grant would have replied that it was not the city he wanted, but the enemy.

Grant was humiliated by Halleck and gave thought to resigning his commission. Only the persuasion of Rawlins and Sherman deterred him. Sherman reminded him that early in the war men called him "crazy" for overestimating enemy strength. Now, his gallant conduct during the battle had won the endless respect of his soldiers and the public. Three horses had been shot from under him, and Sherman had also suffered a gunshot wound of the hand. For the moment, Halleck kept Grant on a short leash, but he defended him in his dispatches to Washington:

> A great battle can not be fought or a victory gained without many casualties.[156]

Grant moved his headquarters to Memphis on June 23rd, where Julia joined him for a two-month visit.[157] Memphis had recently fallen to the Union, following a spirited naval engagement. Three weeks later, Grant, accompanied by Julia, returned to Corinth, where he learned that Halleck had been summoned to Washington to serve as General-in-Chief, a reward for the successful Western campaigns. Although Halleck and Secretary of War Edwin M. Stanton were old adversaries dating from their California days, Stanton was forced to concede that only Halleck's department had shown results.[158] With Corinth now under Union control, Thomas was returned to the Army of the Ohio, and Grant was given back the Army of the Tennessee.

Once again, fortune favored Grant. By reason of seniority, availability and Lincoln's furtive support, Grant was given command of the newly formed Department of Tennessee, comprising all territory between the Mississippi and Tennessee Rivers, and as much of Mississippi as could be digested. Buell and his Army of the Ohio returned to Tennessee.

Julia and the children remained in Corinth through August 1863.[159] They were housed in the comfortable home of a rebel planter who had been imprisoned for disloyal activities. A cavalry company guarded the area.[160] Thereafter, she returned to St. Louis to attend to the children's schooling.

There ensued many months of relative inactivity as Grant shifted his command around Tennessee. Since supplies could not be carried on the Tennessee River because of the falling water level, the command had to rely on the rail link from Columbus. To protect this route, nine Union divisions were widely dispersed. The enemy usually struck small Union detachments, but in October 1862 they attacked in strength at Iuka and Corinth, while Grant and his staff were in La Grange, Tennessee. General William Rosencrans, a subordinate Union commander, repulsed the assaults, but squandered a golden opportunity by failing to pursue the enemy.

Rawlins was outraged at Rosencrans' apparent gross neglect. Both he and McPherson urged Grant to remove Rosencrans from command, and they even tried to enlist the aid of Julia,[161] who had since rejoined her husband; but Grant took no action. Nevertheless, Rosencrans fell in his esteem. Grant showed no remorse when Rosencrans was ordered to the Army of the Cumberland to replace Buell, who had campaigned unsuccessfully in east Tennessee.

Rawlins generally got on well with newspapermen.[162] Sylvanus Cadwallader, a reporter from the copperhead *Chicago Times,* had earlier presented his credentials. His predecessor had been highly critical of Grant, who in fact had had him imprisoned for falsely reporting the arrival of a Confederate fleet of English-built gunboats. Rawlins was hospitable to the newcomer, and even allowed him to have his mail forwarded to headquarters.[163] Moreover, Cadwallader was a Freemason. When Cadwallader complained to Rawlins that some division commanders were suppressing the distribution of the *Chicago Times*, Rawlins saw to it that the ban was lifted.[164]

Cadwallader quickly demonstrated that his mission was to report news, not indiscretions. In time, he acquired first-hand knowledge of many of Grant's encounters with alcohol and later wrote:

> He invariably drank to excess unless someone was with him (whose control he would acknowledge) to lead him away from temptation.[165]

By now, McPherson had been given command of a corps and promoted to major general. Furious at McPherson's promotion, a passed-over brigadier general related to his senator some stories circulating in Grant's command:

> I will now say what I have never breathed. Grant is a drunkard. His wife has been with him for months only to use her influence in keeping him sober. ..When he came to Memphis he left his wife at La Grange and for several days after getting here was beastly drunk, utterly incapable of doing anything. Quimby and I took him in charge, watching him day and night and keeping liquor away from him and we telegraphed to his wife and brought her in to take care of him.[166]

Similar stories continued to circulate, but as long as Grant had the support of Washburne and Lincoln, his situation was for the moment secure.

Among the problems confronting the command were the thousands of liberated slaves that were beginning to accumulate in Grant's department. Grant appointed John Eaton, an army chaplain, to deal with the matter. In November 1862, Eaton set up a huge contraband camp in Grand Junction, Tennessee, which provided the displaced black population with food, tents and medical care. The able bodied among them were hired out for wages to pick cotton or to work as laborers for the Union Army. Later, Grant gave full support to the efforts of Major General Lorenzo Thomas, Adjutant General of the U.S. Army, to enlist Black soldiers in the army.

With Western Tennessee now under military rule, a cotton frenzy erupted in the department. Large quantities of baled cotton had been accumulating, some privately owned and others bearing the CSA (Confederate States of America) stamp. Since the Confederate Government was accepting baled cotton as payment for taxes, it had accumulated 400,000 bales throughout the South, which it used as security for the Confederate bonds offered for sale in Britain and France. Grant and others feared that the Northern money paid for the cotton would find its way into Confederate economy, to be used for the purchase of arms and medicines from abroad. Some money unquestionably did enter the Confederate economy, but most currency remained locally, to support the white population.

Cotton bought in Tennessee at the low price of ten cents a pound, could be sold at one time for fifty cents in the North;[167] and four times that amount abroad. Lincoln weighed the arguments and concluded that the North would benefit from regulated sale of cotton. But he insisted that all purchases be licensed by the Treasury Department.[168]

Grant vigorously opposed the cotton trade, but he assured the secretary of the treasury, Salmon P. Chase:

> No theory of my own will ever stand in the way of my executing in good faith any order I may receive from those in authority over me.[169]

The cotton bonanza attracted hordes of Northern speculators, politicians, army officers, and members of the Dent and the Grant families. Wrote Charles Dana, himself a cotton buyer and later assistant secretary of war:

> Every colonel, captain or quartermaster is in secret partnership with some operator in cotton.[170]

J. Russell Jones, Galena politician and federal marshal, earned a paltry $25,000 during a brief visit to Memphis and Arkansas, under the auspices of a Union general. He complained to Rep. Washburne that he was unhappy with his small profit.[171]

Grant singled out the Jews in the Memphis region as the principal offenders, although it appears from the lists of arrests, trials, etc. that only a small percentage of the names appear to be of Jewish origin. Grant, who had earlier been attracted to the Native American (Know Nothing) Party, was offended when he was approached by Henry and Harmon Mack, Cincinnati manufacturers of tents and clothing, who requested permission to ship cotton. Both were partners of Jesse Grant in the prospective cotton transaction.

Against Rawlins protests,[172] Grant issued his infamous[173] Order #11, expelling all Jews from his department without appeal, in what today would be regarded as a form of ethnic cleansing. The order was later cancelled by Lincoln, but not before thirty Jews and their families in Paducah were forced to leave their city, some in the dead of night. Two of the expelled had served in the Union Army.[174] The 1,000 Jews residing in Memphis were placed on notice, and in Holly Springs several Jewish officers tendered their resignations. Congress was incensed, and motions of censure were introduced, but Rep. Washburne succeeded by a vote of sixty-three to fifty-six in having them tabled. In later years, Grant denied that there was no appeal. He stated that the order had been issued by a subordinate, but like other statements in his memoirs, this was not entirely ingenuous. Wrote Julia Grant:

> General Grant wrote his own reports, his own messages, his own proclamations...[175]

At Grant's headquarters at La Grange, West Tennessee, a first lieutenant in the regular army named James Harrison Wilson reported for duty. A Military Academy graduate,[176] he and his family were friends of Rawlins. Wilson was also a life-long friend of McClernand, with whom he enjoyed exchanging reminiscences.[177] Like Rawlins, Wilson did his best to cement relations between Grant and McClernand; and, like James B. McPherson, he was destined to rapidly rise to high command. Both McPherson and Wilson were professional soldiers and had the talent to work well with the volunteer staff officers. Julia and Mrs. Hillyer were in La Grange at the time.[178]

Rawlins showed Wilson Grant's written pledge and told him plainly:

> I am told you don't drink; but you should know that there are lots of men in this army, some on Grant's staff, who not only drink themselves but like to see others drink, and whenever they get a chance, they tempt their chief; and I want you to help me to clean them out.

He added:

> I want you to know what kind of man we are serving. He's a goddamn drunkard, and he's surrounded by a set of goddamned scalawags who pander to his weakness. Now for all that, he is a good man and a nice man; and I want you to help me [form] an offensive alliance and defend him against the God-damned sons of bitches.[179]

Wilson's rise was predictable. By November 1, 1862 he had been promoted to lieutenant colonel. Grant greatly appreciated his professionalism, which Rawlins and staff could draw upon. But of the services of Rawlins and Bowers, Grant wrote to Halleck that they were "absolutely necessary."[180]

Wilson brought with him the news from Washington that Lincoln had authorized McClernand (over Halleck's objections) to recruit an army for the purpose of capturing Vicksburg. The Confederates controlled 250 miles of the Mississippi between Vicksburg, Mississippi, and Port Hudson, Louisiana, although Union vessels could occasionally slip by their batteries. Since the onset of hostilities, these obstacles had had a devastating financial effect on the farmers in the upper Mississippi and Ohio basins, who had been unable to market their produce in New Orleans. McClernand offered to raise troops in Indiana, Illinois and Iowa for the express purpose of removing obstacles to the free navigation of the Mississippi.

At the time, volunteer units were raised by the governor of the state or by prominent civilians, under the governor's aegis. The rank offered to the commander was determined by the size of the unit raised. In the beginning of the war, captains and lieutenants were elected by the enlisted men, and the field officers chosen by the other commissioned officers. For a period of three months in 1862, the U.S. government attempted to conduct its own enlistments, but thereafter returned the recruiting to the state governors and their politicians.[181]

Wisely, the president had added a proviso to McClernand's orders that his troops may be used for the designated purpose, provided they were not required by Grant.

Meanwhile, Rawlins had received some disquieting news. His ex-partner and childhood friend, David Sheean, a Democrat, whose brother had married Rawlins' sister, Laura, had been arrested in the fall of 1862 for treason, and, owing to suspension of *habeas corpus*, had been imprisoned at Fort Lafayette in New York without a hearing. Thirty thousand Northern citizens were jailed for opposing the war or for giving "aid or comfort to the enemy." Rawlins promptly investigated, then submitted a statement to the secretary of war, accompanied by endorsements by Grant, General John Logan and the Galena contingent at headquarters. The assistance of Representative Washburne was also enlisted. Notwithstanding, the prisoner remained in custody for several months. Rawlins was irate:

> ...the arrest and imprisonment of loyal citizens without trial, I am opposed and shall be opposed to the end of my life.[182]

Halleck was not enthusiastic about McClernand's proposed campaign and preferred that the Vicksburg operation be undertaken by Grant. After receiving assurances of support from Halleck, Grant drew up plans to depart from his base at Grand Junction, Tennessee, march his 40,000 man army south through Holly Springs, Mississippi, to Grenada, and then presumably to approach Vicksburg from the east. Simultaneously, Sherman with 32,000 men would move by ship down the Mississippi River and up the Yazoo River to attack Vicksburg from the base of Walnut Hills, a part of the northern bluffs outside of Vicksburg.

Grant set out in November, following the tracks of the Mississippi Central Railroad south. By the time he had reached Grenada, Mississippi, the enemy cavalry had cut sixty miles of the rail line supplying his troops and had inflicted one and a half million dollars of damage to the Union supply station at Holly Springs. Julia Grant was in Holly Springs with her son Jesse, age four, and her maid Julie, planning to spend Christmas with her husband. Her carriage was burned, but she managed to escape detection.[183]

The destruction at Holly Springs brought Grant's advance to a halt. Without a dependable source of supply, he and his troops were compelled to withdraw. During the return, his men lived first on half-rations and then off the land. Grant carefully noted how well the farmland sustained his army.

Unaware that Grant's campaign had been aborted, Sherman and his troops proceeded up the Yazoo River to Chickasaw Bayou, ten miles north of Vicksburg, where on December 29th they suffered a devastating defeat when his troops failed to scale the fortified heights. His corps had sustained 1,700 casualties; the enemy, 187.

At this point, McClernand appeared with his new army. Believing that he had an independent command, McClernand co-opted Sherman's troops for an attack on Arkansas Post (Fort Hindman) on the Arkansas River, which had been menacing the Mississippi traffic. The attack on Arkansas Post succeeded. Five thousand Rebel soldiers were captured and the Mississippi cleared of yet another Confederate obstacle. Grant was furious when he heard the news, but eventually even he conceded that the effort was useful. Later, he incorporated McClernand into his command and made him a corps commander.

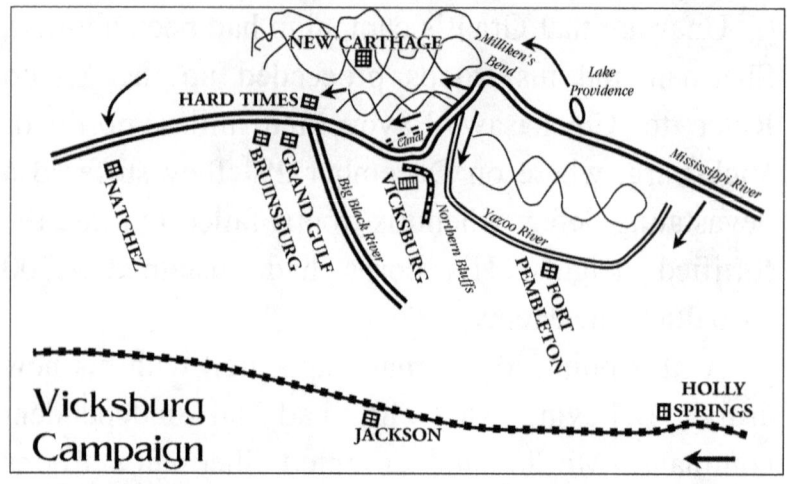

Vicksburg Campaign

Grant moved down the Mississippi and in early January 1863 set up headquarters on a riverboat anchored at Young's Point, Louisiana, near Milliken's Bend, which was situated twenty miles above Vicksburg. Wilson was sent to study the topography. He saw Vicksburg, high up on western bluffs, 200 feet above the river. The Mississippi River ran below and formed a hairpin bend with the open end away from the city. This terrain ensured that any Union vessel passing the city would be exposed to enemy fire, while it made the turn in the bend. The high bluffs west of the city extended to the north of Vicksburg (Walnut Hills), where they had prevented Sherman's entrée. Still further to the north are the bayous, creeks, rivers and swamp land, easily flooded in a heavy rain, which made any approach from the north difficult.

Wilson and Rawlins reviewed the situation. By now, Lieutenant Colonel Rawlins was both AAG and chief of staff,[184] with the responsibility of providing answers. One approach would be to put troops ashore on the Vicksburg landing and have them climb the western bluffs; but this was virtually impossible, since Confederate batteries lined the river bank. Lincoln had visited Vicksburg four times in his youth. He knew the terrain and understood that this plan had little prospect of success. Second, they could come up the Yazoo River to some place at the foot of the northern bluffs and try to scale the heights. Sherman had failed in one attempt at Chickasaw Bayou below the Walnut Hills, but there were other places that might be tried. Lastly, they could march the troops along the west bank to a location below Vicksburg and ferry them by steam transports to the east bank, provided that the Union ships could slip by Vicksburg.

This last proposal was entirely feasible, Wilson argued. He had seen river steamships slink past the well-fortified Hilton Head in North Carolina, without the loss of a single vessel. Indeed, two gun boats had already run the batteries at Vicksburg, but one of them was later captured by the rebels. Steam transports, however, were not gunboats.

Rawlins was convinced that the third plan had merit. He discussed it with Admiral Porter, who somewhat hesitantly acknowledged its feasibility. Rawlins often discussed this third proposal with the other members of the staff in Grant's presence. Grant had sat engrossed in his own thoughts, but in fact was absorbing the details.[185] In the meantime, Grant was immersed in his other ventures, which were underway.

For two months Union soldiers and Black contract workers labored to build a mile long canal across the open side of the Mississippi bend, so that vessels could pass through a short cut and detour the Vicksburg batteries. Steam shovels and steam dredging supplemented the manual labor.[186] From the start, Rawlins believed that the canal was too shallow and doubted that it would succeed. "What's the use of a canal unless it can be dug at least fifty feet deeper?" he asked.[187] To make matters worse, the exit was within range of enemy cannon.[188] Work on the canal was halted when rising water from a freshet flooded the ditch.

Around January 1863, an attempt was made by McPherson's corps to dig another canal west of the Mississippi across a levee into Lake Providence, so that vessels could be sent on a 200 miles journey through a network of bayous and rivers into the

Mississippi River below Natchez. This itinerary had been scouted by Colonel William L. Duff, the new artilleryman, and was deemed feasible. The route eventually proved impractical for steamers, not only because of the submerged debris and low water, but also because the route terminated within range of the guns of Port Hudson, then in Confederate hands.

A north Yazoo attempt was made during February–March 1863, under the direction of Lieutenant Colonel Wilson. The aim was to reach Snyder Bluff, a part of the bluffs to the north of Vicksburg and to come up the bluffs onto dry land. The project began with an effort to bring men onto the upper Yazoo River. A levee separating the Mississippi from the inland waterway was blown up, and boats proceeded past the Yazoo Pass and up the Yazoo River. The men used long poles to clear the track of poisonous snakes hanging from the trees.[189] Progress was halted halfway to their goal by impassible rebel fortifications at the hastily erected "Fort Pemberton."

A south Yazoo effort was later made by Sherman and Flag Officer Porter to follow a southern network of bayous and rivers to reach the Yazoo River and the north bluffs. Porter entered the waterways with eleven ships; Sherman marched along the riverbanks. Once again, the rebels managed to obstruct the waterways, and only with the greatest difficulty, did Sherman manage to extricate the boats.

Grant watched helplessly for nine months as one after another of his projects failed. Desertions mounted. Newspapers mercilessly ridiculed the unsuccessful attempts, and public opinion was rapidly turning against Grant. Sherman later wrote of Grant:

> ...if his plan works wrong, he is never disconcerted, but promptly devises a new one, and is sure he will win in the end.[190]

Meanwhile, the army camps were being swept away by floods. Smallpox, measles, malaria and cholera raged among the troops. Aboard the *Magnolia,* the headquarters ship, one of the black laborers had been using a coffin as a bed. When Rawlins discovered that its original occupant had died of smallpox, he berated the man and had the ship fumigated.[191]

Another important newcomer was Charles A. Dana, who arrived in April 1863. Dana had been a journalist with Horace Greeley's *New York Tribune* but had become a cotton buyer in Memphis when he was recruited by the Secretary of War, Edwin M. Stanton, to visit Grant's headquarters and report on Grant's alcohol problems. Ostensibly, Dana was there "to investigate and report on the condition of pay service in the Western armies," but he fooled no one.[192] William L. Duff, the staff artilleryman, wanted to throw him overboard.[193]

Rawlins was quick to size up the situation, and he took Dana into his confidence.[194] He allowed him full access to the headquarters reports and gave him a tent next to Grant's and a horse. No secrets were kept from him. Dana quickly came to appreciate Rawlins' efforts to keep Grant from mischief. He became a steadfast Grant supporter and a friend of Rawlins.[195] He reassured Stanton, but privately stated that Grant's "seasons" of drunkenness occurred only "once in 3 or 4 months" and "never at critical moments."[196] The staff complied with the ban on alcohol, but there was the occasional slip-up. Once, in a fit of exuberance, McPherson, proposed a toast and offered a glass of champagne to Grant, which was refused.

On July 13, 1863 Dana described Rawlins to Stanton:

> ...Rawlins...is a very industrious conscientious man, who never looses a moment and never gives himself any indulgence except swearing and scolding. He is...a townsman of Grant's and has a great influence over him, especially because he watches him day and night, and whenever he commits the folly of tasting liquor hastens to remind him that the beginning of the

war he gave him [Rawlins] his word of honor not to touch a drop as long as it [the war] lasted.

About Rawlins' skill with the pen, he later wrote:

He [Rawlins] is too slow and can't write the English language correctly without a great deal of careful consideration.[197]

Rawlins was fortunate in having Bowers and later Parker on the staff, to help with the literary requirements.

Grant was delighted with Dana's arrival, if for no other reason than Dana sent long dispatches to Stanton, sparing Grant the necessity of a daily report.[198]

Dana had a poor opinion of many on Grant's staff. He found Colonel Clark Lagow "a worthless, whiskey drinking useless fellow...he and Colonel Riggin were neither worth their salt."

Dana further described Rawlins as "one of the most valuable men in the army...he had a very clear mind, clear, strong and not subject to hysterics. He bossed everybody at Grant's headquarters...I have heard him curse at Grant when according to his judgment, the general was doing something that he thought he had better not do. But he was entirely devoted to his duty with the clear judgment and perfectly fearless. Without him Grant would not have been the same man. Rawlins was essentially a good man, though he was one of the most profane men I ever knew; there was no guile in him—he was as upright and as genuine a character as I ever came across."[199] "Damned old skeeziks," was a common Rawlins epithet when Grant was "misbehaving."[200]

At Wilson's urging, Rawlins made several attempts to control his cursing, especially in the presence of women. On one occasion he apologized to Grant. "That's all right, Rawlins," said Grant, "I understand you were not cursing, but…simply 'expressing your intense vehemence' on the subject matter." Grant was referring to a memorable incident when McClernand excused his cursing at one of Grant's orders as merely an expression of "intense vehemence."

The months dragged by, and seven attempts were made to get at Vicksburg, without success. In desperation, Grant convened a conference aboard the *Magnolia*. The spring rise of the Mississippi was expected, which would encumber any approach to Vicksburg through the bayou lands.

Rawlins interrupted the discussion to tell Grant of the route he and Wilson had long been studying,[201] namely running the gunboats and river transports past the Vicksburg batteries and marching the troops along the west bank; then using the vessels to ferry the army over to the east bank. McClernand enthusiastically supported the plan; Sherman, McPherson and Dana were adamantly opposed, since the army would lack draft animals to transport supplies and ammunition from the riverboats. Rawlins would not permit the matter to be dismissed, while Grant listened patiently. In his memoires Grant states that he favored the plan *from the first,*[202] but this was most emphatically not the case. If it were so, he could have implemented the plan at the start.

Rawlins kept Washburne abreast of developments. He even supplied him with opinions as to which generals Lincoln should promote.[203]

In late March 1863, Julia Grant, Fred (age twelve) and Ulysses, Jr. ("Buck," age ten) joined the staff headquarters aboard the *Magnolia*, relieving Rawlins of some responsibility. As Cadwallader noted:

> When the army had a period of repose and inaction and Rawlins was nearly worn out by the eternal vigilance necessary to Grant's salvation, it was noted that Mr. Grant and family invariably visited headquarters for a few weeks...[204]

Julia ate in the mess and visited the sick soldiers. As always, Grant insisted that she spare him the details of the soldiers' infirmities.[205]

At long last, the combined naval and land proposal of Wilson and Rawlins was adopted, after the other options had failed. To divert the attention of the Confederate Army in Vicksburg, a cavalry division under Brigadier General William Grierson, was sent galloping over the length of the Mississippi to Baton Rouge, Louisiana, inflicting damage along the way. Also, Sherman was ordered to make a feint up the Yazoo River to the northern bluffs at Haynes Bluff. By these efforts, Grant hoped to conceal the movement of his army.

A route had to be found on the west side of the river, along which the Union troops could march south. The task was assigned to Generals McClernand and McPherson. The initial forty mile march to New Carthage, Louisiana, presented no great obstacles. "There is a good wagon road from Milliken's Bend to New Carthage," Grant had written to Stanton.[206] Some of the troops boarded skiffs, scows and small river boats, but most marched along wagon roads on corduroyed tracks and over improvised bridges. From New Carthage, both corps had an additional march of forty miles over poor roads and drover trails, along bayous and lakes, to the town of Hard Times on the Mississippi River. Across the river from Hard Times was Grand Gulf, Mississippi, still in enemy hands.

The Union naval run began on April 16, 1863. Seven ironclads, three transports, loaded with forage and supplies, and ten coal barges in tow[207] set out to dash past the heavy guns of the Vicksburg batteries. One hundred soldiers had volunteered for shipboard duty aboard the transports, since the civilian crews had deserted. The superstructures of the vessels were reinforced with bales of hay or logs around the deck. The passage took almost two hours during which time 525 heavy and light artillery rounds, by Dana's count, (111, by another tally[208]) were fired at the flotilla. The vessels were struck eleven times,[209] but all but one transport and six coal barges made safe passage. Ten days later an additional six transports and twelve barges ran the gauntlet. Not a single man died in transit. On board one of the vessels was Colonel Lagow, Grant's bibulous ADC, who declared that he "was satisfied never to attempt such a thing again.[210]

Grant, accompanied by his staff and Fred, traveled by horseback along the route taken by McClernand and joined the army at Hard Times. He had hoped that by now the navy had reduced the Confederate stronghold of Grand Gulf, across the river. Indeed, Union gunboats had tried to silence the heavy guns of the fort, but were badly mauled. Since a crossing could not be made at Grand Gulf, the army marched ten miles further south, on the advice of a slave, who indicated a favorable site for a crossing. The army crossed the Mississippi River on April 10th at

Bruinsburg (on the east bank), and after a day of hectic transport, Grant and his 23,000 Union soldiers were all safe on the east bank—"the same side as the enemy." Three days rations of salt, hardtack and coffee were issued to the troops; for the rest, the soldiers would have to live off the land. The troops found abundant supplies of hog, mutton, beef and vegetables in the rich countryside. Grant had hoped that General Nathaniel Banks also would bring supplies from New Orleans, but this wish was unfulfilled.

One of the plantations belonged to Jefferson Davis. A mount was taken from his stable, which Grant named "Jeff Davis." It became a favorite of Grant and remained with him throughout the war.

Fred Grant accompanied his father until the crossing, and thereafter he tagged along with and without Dana for the next two weeks. Rawlins thought he would have a stabilizing effect on Grant.[211] Julia and Buck had been sent home.

After the safe transfer of Grant's army to the east bank, McClernand was ordered to capture Grand Gulf, so that the Confederate garrison could not threaten Grant's rear; but he found the fort abandoned by the enemy. Sherman was instructed to move his corps south by the same route the other corps had taken and to join Grant on the east bank.

Two Confederate forces opposed the Union army: John C. Pemberton in Vicksburg with 32,000 troops; and Joseph E. Johnston, forty miles from Vicksburg, in Jackson, Mississippi with 12,000 men. Grant resolved to first defeat Johnston's army; next, to sever the railroad tracks supplying Vicksburg; and then, to confront Pemberton.

The march to Jackson was encumbered by the destruction of two important bridges by the enemy. Wilson supervised the repair crews at Port Gibson and later at the North Fork.[212] Rawlins worked alongside the repair crews, swinging an ax, which he used with great familiarity. At the time, he appeared to be in prime health, and as "hardy as any man in the services."[213] His work was never-ending. Every written report passed through his hands, and he reviewed every outgoing order. All this, with the army on the march.

Grant wrote many orders in his own hand. He detailed the routes of march for divisions and smaller units, even specifying the food and tools to be carried. His words were brief, terse and effective. "He used Anglo-Saxon words much more frequently than those derived from the French or Latin tongues."[214] Porter later wrote:

> There was a spur on the heel of every field order he sent.[215]

It was also said:

> There is one striking thing about Grant's orders; no matter how hurriedly he may write them in the field, no one ever had the slightest doubt as to their meaning; or ever had to read them over a second time to understand them.[216]

Many persons credit Rawlins, "but they were in error."[217] Rawlins did insist on verifying every dispatch sent by Grant and rewrote them, if necessary.[218]

Rawlins noted that the army movement was being impeded by the freed slaves crowding the roads. He arranged employment for all over ten years of age, picking and ginning cotton, for which they were paid 12½ cents a pound. The price of cotton promptly dropped to fifteen cents in Memphis.[219]

Instead of directly attacking Vicksburg, Grant advanced to Jackson, Mississippi, forty miles to the east of Vicksburg. On May 14th he defeated the Confederate Army of General Joseph E. Johnston. Military stores were captured, and the important rail line supplying Vicksburg was cut, effectively isolating the city. Two days later, McClernand's corps united with the other two Union corps. They countermarched to Champion Hill, a seventy-five-foot hill midway between Jackson and Vicksburg. There, in a fierce battle, the Union army routed the entrenched army of General Pemberton and drove it across the Big Black River to Vicksburg. Losses were heavy: 1,400 Union and 3,800 Confederate casualties. During the battle, Fred Grant received a wound to the left leg,[220] but the injury was slight[221] and healed without complications. This must have been of great concern to Grant, since gloom still hung over headquarters after the recent death of Sherman's son. After Champion Hill, Fred shared a tent with his father.

As Rawlins, Grant and Dana were surveying the dismal battlefield, strewn with bodies, a wounded Confederate soldier called to them:

> For God's sake, gentlemen, is there a Mason among you?

"Yes," said Rawlins, dismounting. "I'm a Mason."

Rawlins knelt by the dying man, who gave him letters and a trinket to send to his wife in Alabama. Rawlins took the items and left with tears in his eyes. He succeeded in having them sent to the widow.[222]

During the crossing of the Big Black River, Cadwallader saw Grant go into the tent of his artillery officer, Lieutenant Colonel William L. Duff, and ask for whiskey. The officer drew a canteen from under his pillow and gave him several drinks over the next half hour. The officer was known to have a half barrel of whiskey in his tent and often catered to Grant's craving. Dana characterized Duff as an incompetent artillery officer:

> General Grant knows he is not the right person; but it is one [of] his weaknesses that he is unwilling to hurt the feelings of a friend and so he keeps him on.[223]

Duff was later mustered out of the service at City Point.[224] He retained kindly feelings toward Rawlins.

As the army advanced toward Vicksburg, it passed the northern bluffs, where Sherman twice had been halted. A supply train was quickly established at Chickasaw Bayou so that the army could now be supplied from the Mississippi River to the Yazoo River and up the northern bluffs onto dry land.

Lincoln was delighted with the progress of the campaign. To a friend he enthusiastically wrote:

> ...his [Grant's] campaign...is one of the most brilliant in the world.[225]

So far, so good.

McClernand's corps made the initial assault on May 20th on the Confederate entrenchment outside Vicksburg. After achieving slight gains, it was beaten back. For some unaccountable reason, McClernand sent word to headquarters that he had made a lodgment in the Vicksburg defenses. On the basis of this report, Grant ordered a general attack on the Confederate line, but the Union forces were repulsed with severe losses. Rawlins was livid with rage. He ordered Major Bowers to open the record book and charge a thousand lives to that "----------McClernand!"[226]

To add to the ill feelings, McClernand issued a congratulatory order to his soldiers, in which he attributed his failure to smash the enemy defenses to a lack of support. A month later, the newspapers reprinted the message. McClernand's conduct was quite unprofessional, since a corps commander is required to obtain prior approval before any statement can be released to the press. In fact, Grant also had been guilty of a somewhat similar offense. When he first occupied Paducah, he allowed the newspapers to publish his letter to the Speaker of the Kentucky House of Representatives, which had not been cleared by Fremont. For the offence, he received only a mild reprimand.

Rawlins and Wilson were both friends of McClernand and greatly admired his strong traits.[227] They had striven valiantly to maintain harmony between Grant and McClernand.[228] Rawlins had often re-worded orders, so as not to anger McClernand, but now Rawlins could not repress the indignation of Sherman and McPherson at this breech of military conduct. It no longer mattered that McClernand had raised his own troops and had led them competently through the west bank tangle and up Champion Hill.

Grant consulted Halleck who assured him that Grant had full authority to proceed as he wished. Accordingly, on June 17th, Grant suspended McClernand. General McClernand was a brave and able corps commander, but lacking in the loyalty that Grant demanded. McClernand promptly carried his complaints to Lincoln and demanded that Grant's personal and professional activities be investigated. Edward Ord replaced McClernand, and the siege of Vicksburg proceeded harmoniously. McClernand was later returned to duty after Grant was ordered east.

With the failure of the direct assault, a siege was begun and dragged on for forty-eight weary days. The enemy had constructed a formidable entrenchment, with eight miles of well interlaced rifle pits and breastworks around the city, in addition to five miles of waterfront fortifications. Enemy artillery surrounded the city, skillfully positioned to deliver enfilading fire. Among the weapons later captured were 60,000 imported .577 caliber Enfield rifles, considered superior to the .58 caliber Springfield rifle of the Union army.[229] To add to their discomfiture, the Union troops were unused to the heat of the Southern day and to the dampness of the nights.[230] General Robert E. Lee in Virginia doubted that the Union would actively campaign in June. Grant received reinforcements from four other commands, all but guaranteeing a victorious outcome. The new supply route over the northern bluffs assured the Union troops of adequate rations, but within the city, 500 civilians and 31,000 Confederate soldiers were slowly reduced to near-starvation.

Adam Badeau joined the staff as military secretary, at the recommendation of Wilson.[231] Born in Brooklyn, New York, Badeau had been a clerk in the War Department before the war. He had received a wound to the foot at Port Hudson and had recuperated in New York, under the care of John Wilkes Booth and his brother.[232]

On one occasion, Rawlins discovered that Bill Barnes, Grant's servant, had slipped Grant a drink. He had the man strung up by his thumbs and threatened to blow his brains out.[233] When Rawlins became excited he gesticulated vehemently and his expletives exploded.[234] Barnes, none the worse for wear, remained with Grant intermittently throughout the war and several years thereafter.

In early June, Rawlins noticed a change in Grant's speech and writing, He soon found the cause. Grant had been drinking with the surgeon, and Rawlins had found an unopened case of wine outside his tent.

Grant insisted that the wine was for toasting the forthcoming victory at Vicksburg. Rawlins was infuriated and wrote Grant a formal letter:

> Dear General. I have heard that Dr Millan...a few days ago induced you, notwithstanding your pledge to me, to take a glass of wine, and today I found a box of wine in front of your tent...emptied...and the lack of your normal promptness of decision and clearness of expressing yourself...Had you not pledged me the sincerity of your honor last March, that you would drink no more during the war...you would not today have stood first...as a successful military leader....if they [my suspicions] are correctly founded...let my immediate relief from duty in this department be the result. I am, General, yours respectfully, John A. Rawlins.[235]

Early the next morning, before reading the letter, Grant left for a trip to Satartia, fifty miles up the Yazoo River. While he was gone, Rawlins raided the staff tents and destroyed every bottle of wine or spirits he found.[236]

There are three versions of the Satartia trip. The *first* was written by Dana and published on April 28, 1891 (six years after Grant's death) in the New York *Sun*. In it, Grant's alcoholic binge lasted one day, and there was no mention of Cadwallader. In fact, in a letter to Wilson on June 18, 1890, Dana specifically denies that Cadwallader was present. The *second* account was written in 1885 (the year of Grant's death) by Sylvanus Cadwallader, who was then sixty years old[237] and had retired to a sheep ranch in northern California. His account was not published until 1955.[238] In the Cadwallader account, the bender lasted two days and Dana was not mentioned. The *third* account was supposedly written by Dana[239] but in fact was ghost-written by Ida Tarbell, a staff writer for *McClure's Magazine*, who had conducted many lengthy interviews with Dana. Presumably, Tarbell reworded Dana's original 1891 article, but changed Grant's drunkenness to "sickness."

As background to this discussion, it must be remembered that Grant died in 1885 from throat cancer, after a steady decline in his health and fortunes. Throughout his agonizing and lingering illness, the public received daily reports of the suffering endured by their "humiliated, bankrupt and voiceless" general.[240] One and a half million mourners showed up for the funeral parade. An army of salesmen, many wearing Grand Army of the Republic badges, sold 325,000 copies of his memoirs to families less interested in reading the book than in showing their devotion to the memory of their long-suffering hero. Any criticism of Grant had to be circumspect. The Grant family strongly denied any suggestion of alcohol dependence and this sentiment appears to have been accepted by those given access to the Grant papers.

The author has condensed the colorful account of Cadwallader.[241]

Before he had time to read the Rawlins letter, Grant, accompanied by a cavalry escort, left on a steamboat up the Yazoo River for Satartia, where a rebel army was reported to be encamped. Rawlins could not go along, since he was deeply immersed in his staff duties. On the way, the steamboat met another boat, the *Diligent,* aboard which Cadwallader was returning from Satartia, which was still in Union hands. Grant knew the captain of the *Diligent.* He transferred himself and his escort to the *Diligent* and ordered that the vessel return to Satartia. Once aboard, Grant promptly began drinking in the bar. Cadwallader prevailed on the captain to close the bar and ordered the escort officer to bring Grant to his stateroom. In the cabin, Cadwallader saw bottles of whiskey on a table. Over Grant's protests, he threw them out the window into the river and finally got Grant to go to sleep.

When they reached Satartia, Grant ordered the escort officers to take his men and the horses ashore, despite warnings that the town might have been recaptured by the enemy. The reporter got him to go back to bed and the *Diligent* set out for Haines Bluff.

An hour later, Cadwallader discovered that Grant had found another source of supply and was again drinking.

Grant ordered the captain to take him further downriver to Chickasaw Bayou, but this would mean arriving in daylight at a place where the whole command could see him. The scandal might be final and irrevocable, so Cadwallader persuaded the captain to delay the return. Unfortunately, they had tied up alongside a sutler's boat, which stocked a large supply of spirits. Cadwallader instructed the sutler not to serve Grant liquor, but by the time Cadwallader returned to *Diligent*, Grant had already found his way to the sutler's boat.

When Cadwallader finally got him ashore, Grant insisted on riding his horse back to headquarters. The horse, aptly named *Kangaroo*,[242] ran off with its rider. By the time Cadwallader caught up with Grant, he was swaying in the saddle. Cadwallader dismounted him and let him sleep on the ground. He sent word to Rawlins who dispatched an ambulance. When the ambulance returned to Chickasaw Bluff with its two passengers, Rawlins was waiting. By now the drunkenness had worn off. Grant bid Rawlins a cool "good evening" and went into his tent to sleep.[243]

Wilson had some difficulty in fully accepting Cadwallader's account, because of a discrepancy in dates,[244] but the version broadly conforms to the report of Dana. Both Dana and Cadwallader were long regarded as reliable correspondents; but the reader is left to form his own conclusions. We remind the reader that the object of this study is not to *convict* Grant but to assess his relationship to Rawlins.

Meanwhile, Rawlins watched Grant day and night. His admonitions to Grant appear to have been heeded, at least while Rawlins was present.

On July 4th, Vicksburg fell to the Union army, and immediately thereafter, Port Hudson, Louisiana, surrendered to the army of General Banks. At long last, the impediments to Mississippi traffic had been removed. Judged by the number of enemy prisoners, the surrender of Vicksburg was the greatest victory won by an American army, but, of course, Gettysburg, won the same day, had been harder fought.

A question arose as to the fate of the 31,000 Confederate soldiers. Against Rawlins' advice, Grant paroled the rebels and permitted them to return to their homes, there to await exchange. Grant reasoned that he lacked the resources to imprison them or to transport them to Union jails. A few weeks later, the

Confederate government repudiated the terms of the parole, and a number of the rebel soldiers were back again in the Confederate army.

Army discipline required careful enforcement of the military penal code. Numerous Union and Confederate soldiers had been sentenced to death by Union army courts martial and were awaiting execution. Notwithstanding, Grant never hung or shot a prisoner condemned by a military court. In the early days of the war, execution of the prisoner was prohibited unless the sentence had been approved by the president. Later, when Congress authorized execution without presidential approval, the forty-fifty men, whose death sentences were then in pendency, were remanded for execution. Grant ordered Rawlins to submit a brief, querying the propriety of executing a prisoner under Congressional authority, who had been previously sentenced when presidential approval was required. When no answer was forthcoming, Grant ordered the prisoners to be released.[245]

Following the capture of Vicksburg, Grant's commission was changed from Major General of Volunteers (USV) to Major General of the Regular Army (USA). He would now have tenure with pay after the war.

GRANT'S KEEPER

At the time of the Vicksburg surrender, Lieutenant Colonel Rawlins, was described as being five feet seven inches in height with black hair, dark eyes and swarthy complexion. "Black John," Ely Parker called him. He was depicted as "just a plain, blunt man full of purpose and vigor, of austere habits, severe morals, inflexible will, resolution and courage."[246] He worked day and night, never presuming even the slightest familiarity with Grant, whom he always addressed as "General."

John Rawlins (third from left) and Ely Parker (fifth from left)
Library of Congress

Julia Grant joined her husband in Vicksburg. Cadwallader noted:

> When the army had a period of repose and inaction and Rawlins was nearly worn out by the eternal vigilance necessary to Grant's salvation, it was noted that Mr. Grant and family invariably visited headquarters for a few weeks...[247]

Headquarters in Vicksburg was established on the first floor of the twenty-five-room home of Mrs. Anna Maria Lum[248] on South Washington Street and Klein Streets,[249] where it remained for nearly a year. The home was formerly the headquarters of General Pemberton.[250] William Lum, who had died in 1856, had been a successful merchant originally from Pennsylvania, with seven children and a Northern wife. She had employed white women rather than slaves in her household.[251] A Northern governess, a Miss Mary Emmelene Hurlburt ("Emma") from Danbury, Connecticut, had been hired before the war. She had probably attended the Danbury Academy & Young Ladies Seminary and was known to be an accomplished musician and a linguist. The war had stranded her in Vicksburg. By now, her clothes were "pretty thoroughly worn," [252] and she was almost "barefooted."[253]

Miss Hurlburt had been keeping company with a Confederate artillery officer in Withers Battalion, who had perished during the siege.[254] The governess, almost in rags, pleaded to obtain food for the family. Grant had rations of flour, coffee, sugar, tea and bacon issued to the household.[255] She soon became a favorite of the staff. When one of the officers sent her a bouquet of flowers anonymously, Rawlins investigated and discovered that the sender was a married man; whereupon Rawlins ensured that those profligate attentions did not recur.[256] On one occasion, Rawlins saw Miss Hurlburt and the girls riding in an army carriage. He complained to Julia Grant:

> I do not think it just the thing for a United States soldier wearing the United States uniform to be acting as coachman for a lot of rebel women.

Julia Grant did not reply.[257]

After an absence of several weeks while she enrolled the children in a St. Louis school, Julia Grant returned to find a change in the Lum household. Grant explained to her that it started when one day Miss Hurlburt made an appearance in an utterly charming new white apron with her hands thrust in her pockets. Since then, a bewitched Rawlins rode in the carriage with the Lum household.

Rawlins became completely smitten with Mary Emmeline Hurlburt ("Emma"). At the time, he had been a widower for two years. He had a rugged physique and was in apparent good health. After overcoming his shyness, he courted the young lady, and in the fullness of time she consented to become his wife, but on condition that she first return home to Danbury.

While stationed in Vicksburg, Rawlins found employment for a fourteen year old runaway black boy, named Jerry, who remained in his employ as a servant throughout the war and thereafter. Rawlins saw to it that Jerry received a useful education. When Rawlins died, he "had no more sincere mourner than this faithful black boy, Jerry."[258]

Grant decided to give Rawlins a respite from his duties by sending him to Washington, to defend his actions in the dismissal of McClernand and the parole of the Confederate prisoners. Rawlins took with him a three-foot long box containing the names of the parolees.[259]

In a letter of introduction to Lincoln, Grant wrote:

> Sir: The bearer of this, Lt. Col. J. A. Rawlins is the assistant adjutant-general of the Army of the Tennessee…Colonel Rawlins goes to Washington now by my order…Any information desired of any matter connected with this department…he can give better probably than any other officer in it…I know you will feel relieved when I tell you he has not a favor to ask for himself or any other living being. Even in my position it is a great luxury to meet a

gentleman who has no ax to grind and I can appreciate that it is infinitely more so in yours...[260]

Rawlins arrived July 30th and met the following day with the president and his cabinet. Edwin M. Stanton, secretary of war, and Gideon Welles, secretary of the navy, were both Freemasons. The interview was recorded by Welles in his diary:

> Friday, July 31, 1863...[I] was much pleased with him, his frank, intelligent and interesting description of men and account of army operations. His interview ...was of nearly two hours duration and all, I think, were entertained by him. His honest, unpretending and unassuming manners pleased me, the absence of pretension and I may say the unpolished and unrefined deportment of this earnest and sincere man, patriot and soldier pleased me more than that of almost any officer whom I have met.

After Rawlins explained the McClernand situation, Welles wrote:

> In Rawlins' statements there is undoubted prejudice, but with such appearance of candor and earnest and intelligent conviction, that there can be hardly a doubt McClernand is in fault...[261]

When he returned, Rawlins reported to Grant but thought it best not to discuss the trip with the other staff officers.

Another arrival in September 1863 was Ely Parker, Rawlins' close friend from the Galena days, and now a captain. After much difficulty, Parker had at last been able to obtain a commission. He initially was assigned to another command, but Rawlins had him transferred to Grant's staff and made assistant adjutant general. In addition to having the best handwriting, Parker had unshakable loyalty to Rawlins. "Phenomenally strong," he was a good man to have on your side.[262]

It soon transpired that Dana spoke the Seneca tongue. He had been raised in western New York by an uncle who ran a dry goods store which traded with the Seneca. Dana was quick to learn the language. He and Parker often conversed in the Seneca language, especially when they had private opinions to communicate.[263] Parker was usually abstemious, but once a year or so, he would succumb to a bout of heavy drinking.

On August 11, 1863, three weeks after the Vicksburg surrender, Grant appointed Rawlins chief of staff[264] and recommended him for the rank of brigadier general of volunteers, subject to Senate confirmation:

> Lieutenant Colonel Rawlins has been my assistant adjutant general from the beginning of the rebellion. No officer has now a more honorable reputation than he has; and I think I can safely say that he would make a good corps commander. This promotion I would particularly ask a reward of merit.[265]

Bowers became Assistant Adjutant General, and Parker shared the work. Wilson went off to a cavalry command.

Grant wrote to Washburne on August 13, 1863 in support of the Rawlins promotion:

> Rawlins especially is no ordinary man. The fact is had he started in this war in the line instead of staff, there is every probability that he would be today one of our shining lights...[266]

The Vicksburg campaign had raised Rawlins "to the rank of military advisor and strategist in which ...he was destined to the end of the war to exert a powerful influence over the plans and policies..."[267]

Since Rawlins lacked command experience, the Senate was glacially slow to confirm the nomination. Grant later[268] wrote them:

> I would most respectfully but earnestly ask for the confirmation of Brigadier General John A. Rawlins by your honorable body... He comes the nearest being indispensable to me of any officer in the service. But if his confirmation is dependent on his commanding troops, he shall command troops at once...[269]

Until that time, Grant had been regarded as a rather poor respondent by the War Department. His practice had been to write a short statement and turn it over to Rawlins and Bowers for completion, by the addition of dates and figures. Rawlins' appointment to chief of staff helped relieve him of paperwork and gave him more time to plan and advise. Nevertheless, Grant "never transmitted a line of official correspondence, nor made an official report, until Rawlins had examined it carefully and given it full approval."[270] In non-essential matters, Grant was somewhat indolent and did not interfere in affairs that could be handled by Rawlins or others, nor did he oversee his subordinates. If a man failed, he was relieved.[271]

Rawlins was considerate to the staff members and gave each man a sense of worth. He made no effort to conceal his dislike of spirits, but maintained correct relations with the imbibers. His personal habits were austere. He did not drink, nor play cards, nor express settled religious convictions. He had no pretentions and never concealed his humble origins.

To Grant's great regret, Hillyer had resigned in May 1863 because of bad health and returned to St. Louis to resume his practice of the law. George K. Leet and Cyrus Comstock joined the staff, both as aides-de-camp. Comstock was a regular army officer and a graduate of the Academy. Leet had been a clerk and was commissioned a captain when he joined the staff.

Rawlins was anxious to purge the staff of drinkers. Captain Rowley wrote to Washburne in the fall of 1862 that there were four on Grant's staff, Lagow among them, "who I doubt ...have gone to bed sober for a week" and were the reason for Grant's lapses.[272] To rid the staff of the drinkers was no easy matter. Lagow corresponded with Washburne. He had been with Grant from the beginning and knew how to ingratiate himself. Months before, he had presented Grant with a sword that brought tears to Grant's eyes.[273]

In an attempt to halt the illicit traffic in cotton, Grant posted an order temporarily prohibiting the sale or shipment of cotton in the Vicksburg area. A relative of Julia Grant arrived with plans to buy and ship cotton. When Grant directed Rawlins to suspend the order for the benefit of his relative, Rawlins let fly a torrent of violent speech, finally declaring that if he were in command and a relative of his had violated an order, he would hang him! Rawlins later regretted his language and attempted to apologize, but Grant, who had taken no offense, told Rawlins to inform the relative that "his health required him to take the first steamer to Cairo."[274]

A military disaster had been brewing in southern Tennessee. After six months of relative inactivity in central Tennessee, General Rosencrans, now Commander of the Army of the Cumberland, had been ordered to seize Chattanooga, Tennessee, an important rail center. To defend the city, Jefferson Davis sent James Longstreet and his formidable corps to reinforce the Confederate Army. At the time, Grant could do little to aid Rosencrans, since much of his army had been dispersed after the fall of Vicksburg, with McClernand's old corps assigned to General Nathaniel Banks in New Orleans. However, heeding a directive from General Halleck, he sent Rosencrans whatever troops could be spared.

In late August 1863, Grant left for New Orleans to confer with General Nathaniel Banks, Commander of the Department of the Gulf. He was accompanied by Lorenzo Thomas, the Adjutant General of the U.S. Army, who was visiting the Western Theater in order to encourage recruitment of 100,000 black troops in the Mississippi Valley. Grant was hopeful that General Banks might reinforce Rosencrans, but instead, Banks was ordered elsewhere.

Rawlins had vehemently opposed Grant's trip, since he could not accompany him. He remained in Vicksburg, in virtual command of the Department. To ensure continuity of command, Sherman and McPherson yielded seniority.[275]

While in New Orleans, Grant attended a grand review which included McClernand's old Corps, followed by an excellent luncheon, with music, wine and fine food. On the way back to New Orleans,

Grant rode an unusually spirited stallion, given him by General Nathaniel Banks. The horse shied at the approach of a train or a street car and fell on Grant, rendering him briefly unconscious, fracturing a few ribs and severely contusing his left leg. He was confined to bed for two weeks in New Orleans until the swelling subsided. The staff which had accompanied Grant withheld the news from Rawlins, but he learned about the episode in a roundabout way and suspected the worst.

Grant returned by riverboat to Vicksburg and was carried on a stretcher into the Lum home. Julia and Jesse, their five year-old son, were waiting for him. The other children had been left in St. Louis at the home of Julia's cousin. Julia and Jesse would remain intermittently with Grant for several months.

Rawlins pursued his courtship, although deeply immersed in his staff duties. He declined all invitations to balls, theater or other entertainments. He tolerated no extravagances around headquarters. When Bowers grumbled about the wooden candlestick holders, Rawlins snapped:

> ...they are the connecting link between silver candlesticks and no candlesticks at all![276]

Meanwhile, his fiancée, Emma, had returned home to Danbury, Connecticut. Rawlins kept her informed about the family news. One of the Rawlins brothers was sitting for an entrance exam to West Point.[277] His youngest child, Emily, was staying with his mother in Guilford. Rawlins looked forward to meeting Emma's mother in Danbury. He reflected on his early encounter with Emma in quaint Victorian style:

> It was then and there I <u>loved</u> you, loved you for yourself and felt, nothing heart of hearts, that you were fitted to be the mother of the children of the brightest parent and most blessed among the "angels," not a <u>step mother</u>, but a <u>real mother</u> full of affection for them as of love for me.[278]

In the autumn, a shocking reversal of fortune had occurred in Tennessee. On September 19-20, 1863 the Union Army of General Rosencrans had been severely beaten at Chickamauga. Only the courage and steadfastness of the troops of General George Thomas contained the enemy long enough for the Union army to withdraw to Chattanooga and take up a defensive position. The rebels now encircled the city and had mounted cannon on Lookout Mountain facing the city, to interdict supplies from reaching Chattanooga by the Tennessee River. The only supply route now open was a shaky seventy-five-mile trail over the steep hills, insufficient to adequately supply the 40,000 Union soldiers trapped within the city.

When Grant received word of the Chickamauga disaster, he sent Wilson to Cairo by steamboat to learn the particulars, since there was no direct telegraph line from Vicksburg to Washington.

Wilson brought the reply back to Vicksburg, ordering Grant to proceed immediately to Cairo, with no reason given. Notwithstanding the uncertainty, Grant instructed Sherman to prepare for a move to Chattanooga. On October 10th, Grant, his family, Rawlins and the staff, left by boat for Cairo.

While en route, Rawlins wrote to Emma:

> I have written today to my mother and also to my sister informing them of our acquaintance and engagement and assured them both they would love you as a daughter and a sister. We are now en route for Cairo. Where our next headquarters will be I cannot tell.[279]

From Cairo, the party continued east by railroad to Indianapolis, where they were met by Secretary of War Stanton. Stanton was not altogether impressed by Grant. He accompanied the group to Louisville, without revealing the purpose of their trip. Julia and Jesse left in Louisville to visit with Julia's aunt and uncle. Rawlins wrote to Emma about his efforts to ban drinking during the trip:

> Thus far, all have got along without whiskey being under the ban of Headquarters, where I shall keep it.[280]

At Louisville, Stanton divulged the perilous situation in Chattanooga. The Army of the Cumberland was trapped and in imminent danger of starvation or surrender. He ordered Grant to proceed there without delay. Grant was given command of the newly created Department of the Mississippi (Department of the Cumberland and Department of the Tennessee), and with it, the authority to retain or dismiss Rosencrans. Grant chose the latter and made George Thomas the temporary commander of the Army of the Cumberland.

Grant and staff journeyed to Bridgeport, Tennessee, the closest station to Chattanooga still in Union hands. There they met Generals Joseph Hooker and Oliver O. Howard, both of whom had been sent to reinforce the Union forces shut up in Chattanooga. Hooker had completed the longest and swiftest large-scale military movement thus far in the nineteenth century. He and his 20,000 men, together with artillery, horses and impedimenta, had travelled 1,200 miles from Virginia through Indianapolis to Bridgeport, Tennessee. Sherman had not yet arrived.

Dana was there to meet Grant and the staff. He, too, had been in Chattanooga and confirmed his misgivings about Rosencrans' performance. As Lincoln had best summed it up:

Rosencrans is confused and stunned, like a duck hit on the head.

Rosencrans made a brief appearance at the change of command, to further explain the situation. Although Rosencrans was exceedingly popular with his troops, Grant had taken a profound dislike to him.

At sunrise, Rawlins lifted Grant up and deposited him in the saddle, then fastened his crutch behind the cantle. The party proceeded by horseback along the circuitous seventy-five-mile trail over Raccoon Mountain and Walden's Ridge to Chattanooga, on the same fragile route that kept the Union army supplied. Rawlins called it "the roughest and steepest ever crossed by army wagons or mules."[281] Along the trail were the corpses of 10,000 horses and mules.[282]

Roving Rebel cavalry posed an ever-present threat. Grant seldom used a military escort. He preferred the company of his staff and relied on Parker to warn of danger.[283] The terrible thirty-six hour ride was made in torrential rain through deep mud and over dangerous fords. Rawlins dated the onset of his lung troubles to the exposure on that trip. To add to their miseries, the horse Grant was riding slipped and fell on him, bruising the same leg that had been injured in New Orleans.

Grant arrived on October 23rd in Chattanooga, where he met General George Thomas. Thomas, it may be recalled, had relieved Grant after Shiloh, and Grant did not easily forget. Their relations got off to a bad start. Grant was soaking wet when Thomas received him, and Thomas made no effort to attend to his condition until Wilson angrily called for dry clothing. Thomas, a Virginian and regular army officer, was somewhat magisterial in appearance and made Grant feel ill at ease in his presence.[284] Rawlins, as usual, did his best to smooth relations.

First concern was an adequate supply line. Chattanooga was shut in by a chain of enemy emplacements. To the left of the enemy position was Lookout Mountain, a 1,000 foot headland extending to the Tennessee River, on whose summit a strong Rebel battery had been posted, which dominated the approaches to the city by the Tennessee River. In the center, facing the city, was the 300-foot high Missionary Ridge. Here the enemy also had scattered artillery and prepared positions up and down the height. At the right end of the enemy position was Tunnel Hill, actually a part of Missionary Ridge, held by a strong Confederate division.

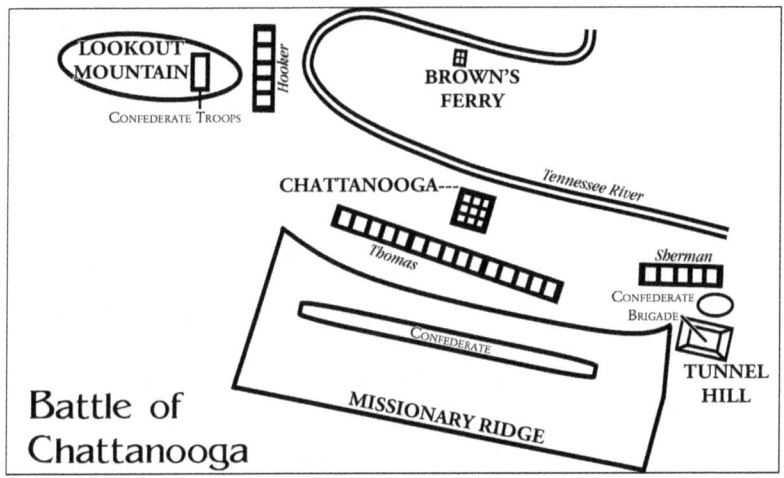

Battle of Chattanooga

General William F. (Baldy) Smith, then a staff engineer for the Army of the Cumberland and an acquaintance of Grant from the West Point days,[285] had devised a plan to relieve the city, but General Thomas had not put it into execution, pending Grant's arrival. If the rebel battery guarding Brown's Ferry across the river from Chattanooga could be taken, then river traffic could come up the Tennessee River to a point three miles below Chattanooga; and from there supplies could be carried by wagon into the city.

The plan was adopted and swiftly executed. A force of 1,500 Union soldiers paddled up the Tennessee River on pontoon-transports and captured Brown's Ferry. Another detachment captured the enemy battery overlooking the ferry and constructed a pontoon bridge. Meanwhile, Hooker's troops blocked rebel reinforcements and dug defensive entrenchments. The foray was fiercely contested and four hundred casualties were sustained, but it opened up a supply line to the railroad terminus at Bridgeport. Chattanooga was no longer invested.

While in Chattanooga, Rawlins found time on November 2, 1863 to write a personal note to Emma:

> My own home is in the West, where I expect to remain and raise my family. I have a mother there, kind and good. The youngest of my little ones, the one needing most attention, is with her. My parents are poor and in most humble circumstances, but they are everything to me and will be, while I live and strive to make honorable the life and [?] they have given me. It is to the one with my mother I propose taking the other two. Would you consent to make my father's house, poor and humble as I have [described] it, your house until the close of this terrible conflict?...

To calm her anxieties, he writes:

> Will my mother and my sister love you? Of course they will.[286]

Rawlins also told Emma that once they were married, he would have to remove his other two children from Goshen, where they currently resided. "The reasons necessitating this I cannot write you but will communicate in full when we meet. They are now, however, most kindly treated and neatly and tastefully cared for by their aunt and grandmother."[287]

General Sherman and his corps arrived November 13th after a strenuous march along the Memphis-Charleston Railroad, repairing track as they went. According to a later account of Baldy Smith, Sherman shared a bottle of whiskey with Grant, unknown to Rawlins, and Grant had to be guided to his room.[288] The following day, Rawlins wrote Washburne, "the General is all himself and in splendid health."[289] This is a reminder that the somewhat naive Rawlins never quite plumbed the depths of Grant's drinking or if he did, he was not about to divulge the details to anyone but Grant. At any rate, Rawlins wrote Grant a blistering letter, but did not deliver it. Instead, he lectured him on the need for sobriety.

Later that night, Grant and Rawlins came upon an all night drinking party, arranged by Colonel Clark Lagow, the ADC. Whiskey had been contributed by a cousin of Julia, who was visiting Grant, and who had also brought some Kentucky wine, sent to Grant by his mother. All this, was witnessed by General Thomas.

The next morning, the greatly embarrassed Lagow was encouraged to resign. Even before the party, Dana, in a letter to Washburne, had recommended his discharge.[290] "Rawlins sometimes acts ugly," concluded the relative who had brought the alcohol.[291]

Rawlins had planned to go on leave so that he could marry, but was now unsure.

> Today, however, matters have changed and the necessity of my presence here made almost absolute by the free use of intoxicating liquors at headquarters which last night's development showed me had reached to the general commanding. I am the only one here (his wife not being with him) who can stay it in that direction and prevent evil consequences resulting from it. I had hoped, but it appears vainly, his New Orleans experience would prevent him ever again indulging with this his worst enemy.

He told Emma that he would try to persuade Grant to send for Julia.

> If she is with him, all will be well and I can be spared...What I have said of the general is strictly confidential.[292]

Meanwhile, Emma informed Rawlins that she was unwilling to live with his parents and his children, unless he was there too.[293] Accordingly, he made arrangements to rent his former house on Hill Street, which had been vacant since he left. "How will this suit my dearest Emma?"[294]

On the eve of battle Rawlins wrote to Emma of his admiration for his chief:

As a commander of troops in the field he [Grant] has no superior. This simple, honest and confiding nature unfits him for contact with the shrewd civilian who would take advantage of unsuspecting honesty. Hence my aversion, as you remember, to having headquarters in cities.[295]

On November 24, 1863 Grant ordered an attack on Bragg's position surrounding Chattanooga, beginning with a double envelopment. The plan called for Hooker and his corps to divert rebel attention with an attack on Lookout Mountain, to the left of the Confederate position. Early in the morning, the mountain was shrouded by fog ("The Battle above the Clouds"), but towards afternoon the mist cleared, and the Union troops could be seen streaming up toward the summit. The fighting lasted the day. By nightfall, the Confederates had evacuated the mountain and fallen back to Missionary Ridge.

That same afternoon Sherman occupied a small hill, believing it to be the foothill of Missionary Ridge. The following day Sherman extended his attack to the Confederate right wing on Tunnel Hill, a part of Missionary Ridge, but, to his horror, he saw that the hill he had occupied the previous day was merely a detached spur. When he tried to mount Tunnel Hill, he encountered fierce opposition, and his troops were repeatedly beaten back. After five hours of furious battle, Sherman was unable to advance further.

Grant and his staff watched the battle from a small knob, about two miles from the base of Missionary Ridge. Thomas' men were strung out along the base of Missionary Ridge, but little was expected of them.

Rawlins pondered the next move. The staff agreed among themselves that Thomas' four divisions should make a demonstration against the enemy rifle pits at the base of Missionary Ridge, in an effort to ease enemy pressure on Sherman. Rawlins proposed this to Grant, who, in turn, suggested it to Thomas. Thomas said nothing and continued to peer through his binoculars. As time passed, Rawlins grew impatient and demanded that Grant issue an order. Grant told Thomas:

> Order your troops to advance and take the enemy's first line of rifle pits!

Thomas' 20,000 troops rushed the rifle pits and overcame the rifle and cannon fire at the base of the mountain. Then, without orders, they began climbing the 300-foot mountain. The soldiers understood what the generals did not immediately perceive, that were they to remain in the rebel rifle pits, they would be exposed to enemy fire from rebel positions higher up the mountain. After capturing the rifle pits, they continued up the heights, with their bayonets reflecting in the sun. They had to rely on bayonets, since they could not load their rifles while climbing. The enemy cannon could not be directed downward, since the angle of declination was excessive, nor could rebel troops fire their rifles from above, for fear of hitting their own men.

Grant watched, as the Union troops climbed the mountain, with little confidence that they would succeed. But the men continued to scramble up. Sheridan's infantry division made the first (?) lodgment on the summit[296] and took 2,000 prisoners. The rest of the enemy withdrew in full retreat down the far side of the mountain.

Rawlins and the staff were ecstatic. The battle immediately enhanced Grant's reputation, dispelling all previous reservations. "Neither he nor the rest of the staff knew why Grant succeeded; they believed in him because of his success," wrote Badeau.[297] W. F. (Baldy) Smith was made a Major General USV.

Cadwallader wrote:

> It is due to General Rawlins, Chief of Staff, to state that upon this occasion, as upon all of Grant's great campaigns, he [Rawlins] is unquestionably entitled to one-half of the praise, for the strategy. Tactical success was due to others; but no general or broad plan of campaign or pitched battle was ever adapted by General Grant without the unqualified assent and approval of Rawlins.[298]

Although comfortably lodged in a small house which he shared with Colonel William L. Duff, the artillery officer, Rawlins by now had developed a persistent cough. Anxious to leave for Danbury to marry Emma, he was greatly concerned that Grant would resume his drinking. He tried to urge Julia to visit, but she apparently was unable to do so. Emma kept him informed about the wedding plans. He deferred to Emma and her mother the matter of the number of guests, etc.[299]

Rawlins received word from the family of his first wife, who had been caring for the two older children, that they were hesitant to let them travel, because of the cold weather.[300] Rawlins planed a visit to Galena, to see his youngest child, before leaving for Danbury. He discussed with Grant his need for medical leave to attend to his cough, but made no mention of his marriage plans. In the Union Army, leave was granted only for medical reasons or by special permission of the secretary of war. Grant, who suspected the underlying reason, recommended that Rawlins depart as soon as possible, so that he could return before the start of the spring campaign.

Grant used the winter to further harass the enemy. Sherman and his corps were sent to raise the siege of Knoxville. Then in December 1863, Sherman was ordered to attack Meridian, Mississippi, a

Confederate rail terminal and from there to march on Mobile, Alabama. Meridian was captured and 200 miles of track destroyed, but Sherman had to curtail his advance when reinforcements failed to reach him.

On December 23, 1963 Rawlins married Mary Emmeline. Hurlburt, a "school teacher," age thirty, daughter of Stephen Ambler Hurlburt, age sixty-two and Sarah Pret Hurlburt, age sixty-four. The Hurlburts resided in a substantial home on 19-21 Franklin Street. Stephen Hurlburt was a fur-blower by trade, one of the craftsmen needed in the manufacture of fur hats, which was the leading industry in Danbury. He had been prominent in the trade, ever since 1849 when a Mr. Nathan Benedict of New York installed a new fur-blowing machine in the Hurlburt factory.[301]

In the New Year, Grant left Chattanooga and traveled through the Cumberland Gap to Lexington and then by train to Nashville, where he established his winter headquarters. Parker, Joe Bowers, and George Leet eluded the roving rebel cavalry and visited the Hermitage, Andrew Jackson's home, where they met Andrew Jackson Donelson, Jackson's adopted Creek son. At the time, Grant was examining the feasibility of marching his Western army along the French Broad River into North Carolina, and from there across that state to the Atlantic Ocean.[302]

Rawlins reported to Nashville in early January. He arranged for his wife and three children to visit for three weeks and lodged them in a small house. During the next three years, he and Emma would have three children of their own, but all died in infancy.

Word reached Grant in January 1864 that Fred was critically ill in St. Louis with "typhoid pneumonia." At the time, Julia was away in Louisville, but when informed, she departed immediately for St. Louis.[303] Grant turned over the command to Rawlins and he too left for St. Louis.[304] Fortunately, the boy's condition had much improved by the time Grant got there.[305] While in St. Louis, Grant found time to attend a banquet held in his honor. With all eyes on him, he refused the offer of a glass of wine. "I dare not touch it," he explained to a friend. "Sometimes I can drink freely without any unpleasant affects; at others I could not take even a simple glass of wine."[306]

Rawlins was greatly concerned when news of the banquet reached him. He wrote to Emma:

> You are fully aware of my fears in all this. I need not state them.[307]

Also, he told her:

> Grant may appear awkward at these affairs, but he likes them nonetheless.[308]

The following month Julia joined Grant in Nashville.

While in Nashville, Grant began work on the Chattanooga battle report. He wrote a simple narrative and handed it over to his staff for completion. The task should have been the concern of Bowers, the assistant adjutant general, but Rawlins insisted on reviewing and approving every line. The final account was accurate and attempted to be unbiased. Rawlins wrote admiringly of Grant's report:

> It is full and complete, written in his [Grant's] usual narrative style, void of pomposity or parade.[309]

Although the battle report was framed with a "scrupulous regard to the truth," it did not do justice to General George Thomas. Grant and Rawlins both believed, incorrectly as it turned out, that Sherman's strong attack on the Confederate right wing had drawn rebel reinforcements from the center and so weakened the center that an advance by Thomas was made possible. The report gave excessive credit to Sherman at Thomas' expense. Later, it was shown that the enemy did not move troops from center to right. In short, Thomas' men had succeeded, where Sherman's had failed. Despite this, Grant did not recommend Thomas for a major generalship in the regular army. Hooker, too, was given insufficient praise for the stunning advance up Lookout Mountain and for the brilliant deployment from Virginia to Tennessee.

Unlike the prevailing custom in other commands, headquarters did not issue florid congratulations to the troops or to the press.[310] Such was not Grant's manner. He and Rawlins were "plain, straightforward, earnest and patriotic men, working together with all their faculties between them, no jealousy, no suspicion and no misunderstanding...Grant was the experienced, unpretending, educated soldier, while Rawlins the civilian was his complement..., rather than the 'power behind the throne.'"[311]

In Washington a bill to revive the rank of lieutenant general was introduced in the House by Rep. Washburne. George Washington had held the rank for one year, and Winfield Scott had received the brevet rank.[312] Rawlins immediately informed Washburne that if three stars meant being taken out of the field, Grant did not want them.[313]

James Wilson, now a brigadier general in the Cavalry Bureau in Washington, kept Rawlins informed of the gossip floating around the capitol. The consensus was that Grant was sorely needed as general-in-chief to settle the strategy and direction of the war; that Halleck was timid and selfish; that the president and his cabinet were pulling in opposite directions. Wilson also recommended that, as a precaution, Grant indicate his disinterest in the presidential office.

In his reply to Wilson, Rawlins stated that "if there is a man in the United States who is unambitious of such honor [the presidency] it is certainly he [Grant]..." However, it would not be wise for Grant to make that statement. Were Grant to deny an intention of running, it "would place him much in the position of the old maid who had never had an offer declaring 'she would never marry.'"[314] Wilson circulated the letter, and it seemed to satisfy the doubters.

With only nine months remaining before the presidential election, Lincoln continued to be apprehensive. He consulted J. Russell Jones, the Galena factotum, who assured the president that Grant had no political aspirations; and Dana confirmed this. Grant gave similar assurances to Washburne.[315] Grant asserted that his only political ambition was to become mayor of Galena long enough to get a sidewalk built from his house to the railroad station.

The bill establishing the lieutenant generalship passed the Congress and was signed into law on March 3rd. With the rank, came the office of General of the Armies of the United States. Lincoln sent for him. Grant had no desire to come east. He continued to believe that the western armies held the key to final Union victory, and he had accepted the third star on the tacit condition that he could continue to serve in the field. Disturbing stories were circulating about the factions, cliques and jealousies within the Army of the Potomac and its predictable hostility to the arrival of any newcomer. In fact, Grant had recommended either Sherman or Baldy Smith to command the Army of the Potomac.[316]

Grant had already decided that if he were compelled to come east, he would not remain in Washington, but would follow the Army of the Potomac into Virginia.

In preparation for the trip east, Rawlins closed the headquarters and sent his wife and children to Galena.[317] Grant wrote to Sherman and McPherson, handsomely acknowledging their contribution to whatever success Grant had attained. Sherman replied[318] bluntly that Grant's ignorance of strategy, science and history might prove a fatal deterrent, but that his common sense seems to have compensated for his deficiencies. "For God's sake and for your country's sake come out of Washington," he advised. Remain in the West and exploit the military opportunities.[319]

Brigadier General John A. Rawlins
Brady-Handy Collection, Library of Congress

WAR IN THE EAST

While en route to Washington, Rawlins had second thoughts about his qualifications for the chief of staff to the General of the Army. He offered to resign, in favor of a more "educated and finished soldier."[320] Grant dismissed his fears.

Grant arrived in Washington March 8, 1864 to receive his commission. He was accompanied by Fred, now fourteen years old, and by Rawlins and Lieutenant Colonel Cyrus B. Comstock. Comstock was a regular army officer, who had joined the staff after Vicksburg. Grant remained only two days in Washington,[321] long enough to requisition any underemployed troops idling in the northern cities. At dinner with Secretary Seward, Rawlins requested that wine not be served. He wrote Emma:

> You know where I am wine is not drunk by those with whom I have any influence.[322]

They returned to Nashville and discussed final plans with the senior commanders. Sherman was ordered to prepare for a march on Atlanta. He was given command of the entire western theater (Division of the Mississippi), and McPherson, his subordinate, the command of the Army of the Tennessee. Philip Sheridan was informed that he would be assigned a cavalry corps in the Army of the Potomac. Prior to this, Sheridan had had only five weeks of cavalry duty.

On March 23rd Grant and staff returned to Washington, accompanied by Julia and Jesse, whom he installed in a boarding house. At the time, his staff included two military secretaries, four assistant adjutant generals, one assistant quartermaster and five aides-de-camp.[323] All except one of his staff were non-professional soldiers. With a total of fourteen officers, the staff was smaller than the staffs of some divisions.[324] General Robert E. Lee, by contrast, had a staff of three officers.

The non-professional (volunteer army) staff officers included Brigadier General Rawlins (chief of staff) and Captain Ely Parker (secretary), Colonel William R. Rowley (AAG), Major Joseph Bowers (ADC), Lieutenant Colonel William L. Duff (artillery), Lieutenant Colonel Adam Badeau (secretary) and Captain George K. Leet (ADG). The only regular among them was Lieutenant Colonel Cyrus Comstock (senior ADC).

New staff officers would be joining Grant, among them Lieutenant Colonel Frederick Dent (ADC), his brother in law; Colonel Horace Porter (ADC), and Lieutenant Colonel Orville E. Babcock[325] (ADC), nephew of J. Russell Jones. All three were graduates of the Military Academy. Also members of the staff were Captain Peter Hudson (ADC) and Lieutenant William M. Dunn, age nineteen, soon to be ADC to Rawlins.

Dana, who knew the staff from the Vicksburg days, long had reservations about its efficiency:

> If General Grant had about him a staff of thoroughly competent men, disciplinarians and workers, the efficiency and fighting quality of the army would soon be much increased. As it is, things go too much by hazard and spasms; or, when the pinch comes, Grant forces through by his own energy and main strength what proper organization and proper staff officers would have done already.[326]

Grant had had a lengthy conversation with the president. Quite likely, Lincoln indicated the political desirability of retaining Generals Benjamin Butler, Franz Sigel, and Nathaniel Banks. All three were military hacks, but had important political constituencies. Butler had been a prominent Massachusetts Democrat, and, as a volunteer general, had kept Maryland from falling into the Confederate camp. Sigel had military training in Germany and enjoyed enormous popularity among the German-American population in the Midwest. Nathaniel Banks had been a former Speaker of the House of Representatives and a Governor of Massachusetts. Lincoln may also have indicated his displeasure with General George Meade, the present Commander of the Army of the Potomac, who, in the past nine months, had not launched a significant offensive.

Grant made no mention of strategy,[327] but it was clear that his intentions were twofold: to engage the Army of Virginia in open country and to divide the Confederacy with invasions from the West.

On March 24th Grant, accompanied by Rawlins and Comstock, proceeded to Culpepper Court House in Virginia, where he set up headquarters in a large house. Grant notified George Meade that he would be retained as Commander of the Army of the Potomac, subject to overview. Accompanied by his staff, Grant visited the Corps commanders and watched dutifully as their troops paraded. Observers noted that on one occasion Grant took the salute with a cigar in his mouth.[328] This would be Grant's first encounter with staff officers with aiguillettes, Zouave guards, and foreign observers with spiked *pickelhaube*.

Grant continued the easy familiarity with his staff, but their relations to him became even more formal. Rawlins gave advice, but with the arrival of the regular army contingent, his opinions became more guarded and his relations with Grant somewhat less intimate. He told Wilson that he felt his influence with Grant was not as before in the salad days.[329] Yet, in his own unassuming way, Rawlins had transformed himself into a first-rate military mind. One of his colleagues wrote of him:

> General Rawlins, though he had not the advantages of an early military education and had learned much from more than two years' experience in war, after which the difference in military judgment which had existed at the beginning must have very largely...disappeared.[330]

Grant, like Robert E. Lee, was not an organizer or a great tactician.[331] Once he formulated a plan, he left the execution to his corps commanders, who were thoroughly competent to modify or improvise tactical decisions. This lessened his need for a well organized general staff and left Rawlins to deal more with policy than with operations. Tactics, as such, were left to General George Meade, the Commander of the Army of the Potomac. Nevertheless, Rawlins did insist on numerical superiority before any military venture.[332] "I believe more in the infallibility of numbers than in infallibility of generals, no matter how great their reputation," he insisted.[333] He wrote to Emma:

If I have ever been of signal service to General Grant, it has been in my constant firm advocacy of many large forces against a small one, in other words of always having the advantage of numbers in our side.[334]

A grave problem now confronted the Army of the Potomac. The three-year enlistments were about to expire for 20,000 of the best soldiers in the Union Army. A $400 incentive was offered to encourage reenlistment, (in addition to the state bounty and a thirty-day furlough), but it was feared that many would elect to return home.

Rawlins, by now, was seriously ill. His cough, which had first appeared during the Chattanooga campaign, failed to respond to treatment. A New York lung specialist had examined him during his recent leave, and, according to Rawlins, had assured him that his lungs were fine and that he merely had an irritation of the bronchus. No medical entry ever appeared in his army medical records.

Grant and Meade had their final conference. Both were in broad agreement on policy:

General Franz Sigel (Department of West Virginia) and his 6,000 men would advance down the Shenandoah Valley to wrest control of the valley and interdict the shipment of supplies by rail to Richmond and Petersburg.

General Nathaniel Banks would advance on Mobile, Alabama, the principal Gulf port. After its capture, Mobile would become a supply base for Sherman's army. Earlier, Grant had questioned Banks' capabilities and wanted him replaced, but neither Grant nor Halleck would issue the order.[335] Then, in response to a perceived threat, the plans for Mobile were deferred. Instead, Banks was sent up the Red River to Texas.

Texas was no slapdash assignment.[336] Early in the Civil War, France, Spain and Great Britain had invaded Mexico following the suspension by the Mexican president, Benito Juarez, of the interest payment on the Mexican loans. Great Britain and Spain had since withdrawn their troops, but France remained with its army of 35,000 men, which it used to install Archduke Maximilian as emperor of Mexico. While the attention of the Union was diverted, many feared that the French troops would cross the Rio Grande and join forces with the Confederate Army.

Banks' army fared poorly with their mission. Within a month, his naval vessels were stopped by falling water thirty miles from Shreveport, Louisiana, and his army was halted by stiff enemy resistance. Plans for the Mobile campaign were shelved.

General Ben Butler, Commander of the Army of the James, would proceed from Fort Monroe up the James River to threaten either Petersburg or Richmond. William F. (Baldy) Smith was assigned to General Ben Butler and given command of a corps. Grant, accompanied by Julia and Rawlins, visited Butler and were favorably impressed.

Before joining Butler, Smith on his own initiative voiced his misgivings about Grant's pending overland campaign and submitted his own plan. He proposed that troops be sent by water to Albemarle Sound in North Carolina, where they could sever the railroad lines supplying Richmond. Although this last-minute proposal irritated Rawlins, he showed it to Grant, who brushed it aside. Had it been presented earlier, it might have been considered.

General W. T. Sherman would begin his 110-mile march from Chattanooga to Atlanta, supported by McPherson (Army of Tennessee), Schofield (Army of the Ohio), and Thomas (Army of the Cumberland), totaling 100,000 men. His opponent, Joseph E. Johnston, had 60,000 men (Confederate Army of Tennessee). A master of maneuver, Johnston was expected to conduct a dynamic, mobile defense, fully availing his Army of the features of the terrain.

Grant condensed the Army of the Potomac into three corps, under Meade. The fourth corps

(Burnside) was initially placed under Grant's direct command.[337] Rawlins anticipated dissatisfaction among the corps commanders, but worked conscientiously to smooth ruffled feathers. Sheridan was given a cavalry corps with three divisions, one of which was commanded by Brigadier General James Wilson.

Meade was seven years older than Grant and somewhat loath, perhaps, to take risks or embark on offensive operations.[338] He belonged to the Army of the Potomac establishment, and his staff contained the scions of the nation's prominent families. They regarded Grant as a "rough, unpolished man" of only "average ability, whom fortune has favored." Rawlins, they agreed, understood "no more of military affairs than an old cat."[339]

Grant ordered Meade to begin the overland operation, leaving him and his subordinates to work out the details. The Army of the Potomac had 115,000 men, Lee had 62,000.

The overland campaign began on the night of May 3, 1864 with the crossing of the Rapidan River at two fords. The army followed the same ill-fated route taken by Hooker in 1863. Ahead, lay the "Wilderness," an eighty-eight square-mile area of wild growth, ravines, swamps and stunted oak and pine. The hope was to cross the region in twenty-four hours by quick march on Brock Road, with baggage train following behind. Flankers could not be posted to guard the army movement, because of the dense vegetation.

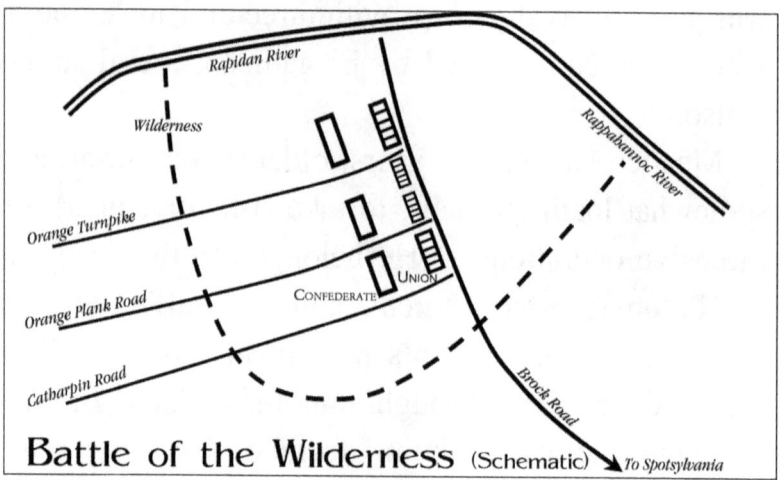

Battle of the Wilderness (Schematic)

The infantry moved slowly, delayed by the baggage train, so that instead of coming onto open ground by nightfall of May 4th, the Union Army found itself still in the savage confusion of the Wilderness. Lee had allowed the Union Army to make the crossing unhindered, but on the morning of May 5th, he brought up his army somewhat perpendicular to the flank of the long train of Union soldiers. This situation could have been a disaster to the Union, had the columns of Confederate soldiers deployed quickly to face the Union line; but the terrain impeded Confederate movement as well.

Lee struck at Grant's right wing; then at Grant's left. There had been widespread feeling among the Union officers, as well as among the rank and file, that Grant did not have the required military talent to defeat Lee and that his victories in the West had been achieved against inferior Confederate forces. After all, Lee had not lost a single battle in Virginia.

Fighting was furious and proceeded at best under regiment or brigade control, each side struggling to gain ground or to turn the enemy's flank. Because of the dense growth, artillery and cavalry were difficult to deploy, and the battle was confined to fierce encounters between smaller detachments.

During the battle both Grant and Meade moved their headquarters, but with the smoke and fire in the underbrush, Grant's party lost their direction. Parker warned them that they were headed toward the enemy and led them back to safety.

News of terrible Union losses kept pouring in, deeply distressing Grant. Outwardly calm and self-possessed, Grant was heard sobbing in his tent. Rawlins and Bowers helped restore his composure. Wrote Wilson:

> I never saw Rawlins in a more resolute or more encouraging temper, or Grant in a state of greater confidence.[340]

During the battle, Grant and Meade conferred frequently. Meade sought Grant's opinion and followed his suggestions. This collaboration would continue throughout the campaign, but Grant gradually assumed a greater role in battle management. Some say that Grant "began to hector and irritate Meade...and to divide with him the tactical control and responsibility for the battle."[341] Another observer had a different impression:

> I do not see that Grant does anything but sit quietly about, whittle, smoke and let General Rawlins talk big.[342]

On the second day (May 6th), the Union left wing succeeded in repulsing the enemy attack, but rebel reinforcements came up the Orange Plank Road to stabilize the Confederate line. The newly arrived Confederate corps commander tried to outflank the Union left wing, but in the confusion, he was shot by his own men. Burnside's corps arrived somewhat tardily, despite Grant's exhortations.[343] Most of his men were recruits, but they contributed to the strength of the Union line. A Confederate attack almost outflanked the Union right wing, but the attack came too late in the second day. The Union commander was able to counterattack and regain ground. Both armies remained in place on the third day (May 7th) and made efforts to retrieve the wounded from the burning undergrowth.

The Union army had suffered a staggering 17,000 casualties, the Confederate 11,000 (?). By now, the troops were debating whether Grant would advance or retreat. Toward evening of the third day, he settled the uncertainty by leading a cheering Union Army south along Brock Road in the direction of Richmond. In the van, they saw a slight figure, seated in a worn saddle[344] on Cincinnati, his 17½ hand bay horse.[345] Next to him rode Rawlins on "General Blair,"[346] a "clay bank" horse named for a friend in the Army of the Tennessee. The drum corps struck up the popular air, "Ain't I glad to get out of the wilderness." Rawlins had to explain to Grant why the men were laughing, since Grant was tone deaf.[347]

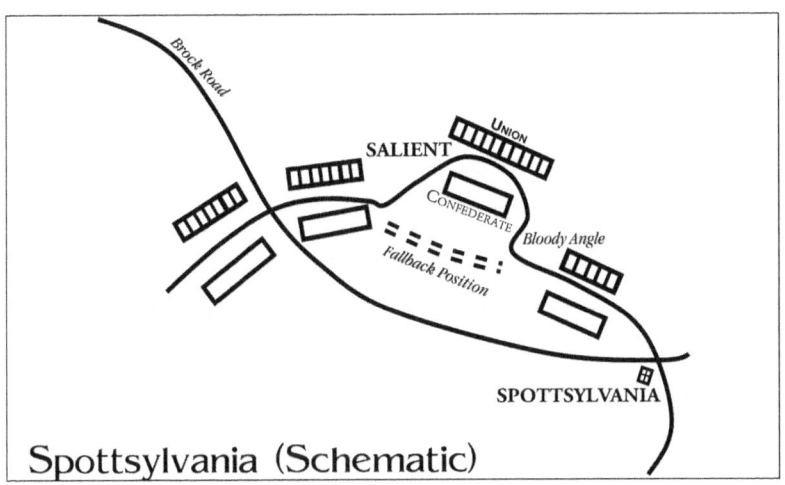

Spottsylvania (Schematic)

Grant's objective was to slip around Lee's right flank and interpose the Union army between Lee and Richmond. This would compel Lee to engage Grant in a stand-up battle, where the preponderance of Union numbers would prevail. Grant's immediate destination was Spotsylvania Court House, an insignificant hamlet twelve miles to the south. Grant hoped to arrive there first, but Lee was faster and unencumbered by a huge baggage train.

A small division (Wilson)[348] of The III Corps (Sheridan) was able in fact to reach Spotsylvania Court House on the morning of May 8th, but had to withdraw for lack of support, so that the enemy was the first to settle in. Meade berated Sheridan for not clearing the road to hasten the army movement. To forestall further complaints, Grant sent the cavalry off on an independent foray against Richmond.

The enemy quickly entrenched behind a four-mile trench with breastworks, the center of which was one and a half miles of elevation called the "Mule Shoe." On this rise, Lee had strategically positioned twenty cannon. A Confederate corps occupied the Mule Shoe, and on either side another Confederate corps was dug in. This was Lee's first major entrenchment.[349] Opposing Lee's position were four Union Corps.

Rawlins wrote to his wife:

> The enemy beat us to Spotsylvania and now hold the place. By this move they have interposed their whole force, perhaps, between us and Richmond. The feeling of our army is that of great confidence and with the superiority of numbers on our side, I think we can beat them notwithstanding their advantage of position.[350]

On the 9th and 10th of May, assaults were made on the Confederate salient, but the line held. On the evening of the 10th, a Union division commander led an attack of twelve regiments which penetrated the Mule Shoe line, but was forced to withdraw with great losses because of the coming darkness and poor support from the other Union corps. On the 11th, battle was hampered by torrential rain, but, as a precaution, Lee constructed a fall-back trench at the base of the Mule Shoe.

On May 11th, Rawlins wrote to his wife:

> Our progress toward Richmond is slow but we are on the way, and do not propose unless some disaster overtakes us, ever taking a step backward...[351]

Grant was more explicit. He wrote Halleck:

> We have now ended the sixth day of very heavy fighting...I propose to fight it out on this line if it takes all summer.[352]

The following day, a furious Union charge by the Union corps in the center captured the salient, but the assault could not be exploited because of rain and insufficient reserves. The Union troops were driven back up the firing steps, over the parapet and into the outer ditch bordering the breastworks. Grant ordered a general assault by the right and left Union wings, but their attack lacked coordination.

By nightfall of May 12th, both armies were exhausted. Around midnight, Grant entered the tent of Colonel W. L. Duff, who was known to keep a half barrel of whiskey. Colonel Duff pulled out a canteen from under his pillow and gave Grant several drinks.[353] Unknown to Rawlins, Duff had long catered to Grant's need for alcohol and continued to do so until mustered out at City Point a few months later.[354]

By the 13th, the enemy fell back to the secondary defensive position at the base of Mule Shoe, which it continued to hold. For the next five days both sides probed and tested their opponent's strength in several sharp actions. The Confederate entrenchment and the enfilading cannon fire had effectively offset the advantage of Union numbers.

On May 18th, the Union army tried another assault but the enemy could not be dislodged. Grant had written to Halleck "I am satisfied that the enemy are very shaky, and are only kept up to the mark ...by keeping them entrenched in every position they take."[355] Union losses were 13,000, including eleven general officers; the Confederates losses are unknown.

Although Rawlins continued to hold Meade in high regard,[356] some of the staff urged Grant to assume direct command of the Army of the Potomac. They argued that Grant's orders lost their piquancy when transmitted through Meade's command. Grant defended Meade, but many thought that Meade was fast becoming a mere chief of staff.[357]

Bad news arrived from the Army of the James. Butler had landed on May 5th at a plantation called "Bermuda Hundred," and promptly dug a defensive entrenchment. At the time, he could easily have taken Petersburg or even Richmond, since the opposition was light.[358] So light, that some defenders had to be recruited from a boy's school and a home for the aged.

Nine days after his arrival at Bermuda Hundred, Butler set out to capture Petersburg, but by then the defenders were better prepared, although still fewer in number. The Army of the James was halted at Drewry's Bluff on May 12th and compelled to retreat to their familiar entrenchments. Thereafter, they contributed little to the campaign beyond serving as a reservoir for reinforcements.

Sigel, too, was in trouble in the Shenandoah. He had been defeated on May 15th at New Market by a smaller enemy force which included 247 cadets from Virginia Military Institute; and compelled to retreat north. Grant sent him reinforcements culled from the idle troops stationed in Washington.

At Spottsylvania, the Union Army disengaged itself the night of May 20th. Suspecting another attempt to outflank him, Lee rushed his men south toward the South Anna River, arriving May 22nd. He crossed the river and promptly entrenched. The "King of Spades," his soldiers called him. He laid out his position in the form of an inverted "V", with the apex touching the river. One Confederate corps was stationed to his left; and another two corps to the right.

Rawlins wrote on May 26th, marveling at the speed with which the enemy put up entrenchments. "…he [the enemy] succeeded in getting here about twelve hours in advance of us and throwing up rifle pits in defense. A few hours always suffice for an army acting purely on the defensive to fortify itself and the fortification make up greatly for inferiority of numbers."[359]

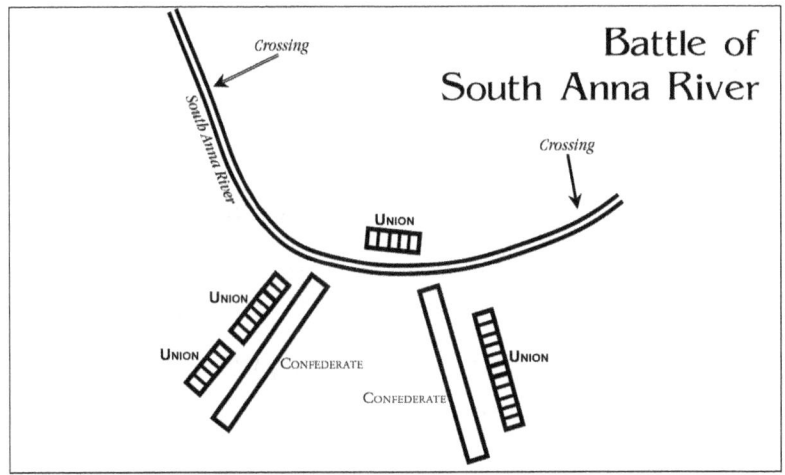

Two Union corps crossed the North Anna River at a hotly-contested bridge and took position facing Lee's left wing on May 23rd. A third Union corps crossed at another bridge and took up a position on Lee's right wing. A fourth corps remained on the north bank of the river, but this corps was not of the best quality and little was expected from it. The Union corps commanders almost fell into Lee's trap while crossing the bridges, since their troops were especially vulnerable and could not have been easily reinforced. Fortunate for the Union Army, Lee was ill at the time, and did not spring his trap. Instead, the Union corps had time to entrench.

Grant soon realized that Lee had outmaneuvered him. With the inverted "V" formation, Lee could shift forces effortlessly to either side, while Grant was unable to reinforce a line with first-class troops without crossing and re-crossing the South Anna River, a marching distance of twenty miles. For two days neither army would initiate the attack, both declining to engage.

On May 25th Grant re-crossed the North Anna River to its northern bank and proceeded south east along the Pamunkey River, a branch of the South Anna. Grant ordered W. F. (Baldy) Smith's corps in the Army of the James to link up with him along the Pamunkey River. The staff debated whether Lee would make another stand before Richmond. Rawlins wrote Emma that he thought they would.

Grant once again tried to outflank Lee. By this time the relations between Meade and Grant teams had become somewhat strained. Grant insisted that the Union objective was not merely to pursue the enemy from one entrenchment to another but to defeat him, no matter the cost.[360]

As Rawlins had predicted, the need for replacements was becoming increasingly urgent. "Reinforcements are still coming forward with commendable promptness. I have every confidence if the Government will keep up this army to its present number, all will go well." [361] Grant had already lost 35,000 men since the crossing of the Rapidan and 20,000 more were about to be sent home at the expiration of their enlistments. To compensate for these losses, Grant stripped Washington of its "homesteaders." Six thousand artillery troops stationed in the city were transferred to the Army of the Potomac to fill the ranks of the infantry.

Rawlins remained optimistic. Two days later, he wrote from Hanover Town, Virginia:

> Unless some terrible blunder is committed in the movements of our army, by which the enemy obtains an advantage over us, Richmond must fall...Of course, our numbers are greater than those of the enemy, but by his fortification he has made up for inferiority of numbers.[362]

On May 29th he wrote:

> My opinion is that, most likely he will defend his new position as long as he can make it tenable, but the prevalent opinion is that he will give it up and retire behind the Chickahominy.[363]

Grant shared Rawlins' optimism.

> Lee's army is really whipped...I may be mistaken, but I feel that our success over Lee's army is already insured.[364]

Despite the demands of his duties, Rawlins took the time to reassure his wife about his health. On May 30th he wrote, "My health is still improving." On the next day, "Colonel Bowers is in very poor health and goes to Washington tomorrow...I am really almost well."[365] But on June 8th he wrote that he had caught a cold, and his cough had returned. Compared to the headquarters of his corps commanders, Grant's headquarters was Spartan. His had a few tents, portable field furniture and simple food.

Still determined to outflank the enemy and come between Lee's army and Richmond, Grant and the Army of the Potomac came to Cold Harbor, six miles from Richmond. Sheridan's cavalry arrived on May 31st and promptly engaged the enemy scouting parties with their new seven-shot Spencer repeating rifles. The Union cavalry had to dismount before they could use their carbines, whereupon the advantage of the repeating carbine was then offset by the greater range of the enemy rifle fire. The following day, Confederate army began to arrive and promptly entrenched along a sturdy five mile line, topped with log breastworks.

Baldy Smith and his 16,000-man corps were among the first Union troops to arrive on May 31st. Weary after a frightful night march from Bermuda Hundred and distracted by the wrong destination given him by Rawlins,[366] his corps did not appear until afternoon.[367] The other Union corps soon followed. On June 1st, some Union assaults were made with slight gains, but rain forestalled a general attack. By the next day, both sides had entrenched along what quickly became a seven-mile front.

Lee had constructed an ingenious, interlocking, zigzag trench with breastworks and deadly enfilading artillery. Such field works quadrupled the strength of the defenders. A shallow trench for kneeling riflemen could be dug in one hour; a solid line of rifle pits in one day; deep trenches with a parapet in two days; and entrenchments with abatis in three days (if wood were available).[368] Slowly, the new rule of thumb was emerging, that if the enemy held an entrenched position for six-eight hours before the arrival of the Union troops, the position would be difficult to capture.[369]

Grant now had the choice of attacking a strongly entrenched enemy or attempting another flanking maneuver. Rawlins vigorously opposed a direct attack, but some of the professional staff, Comstock among them, differed. Grant chose to attack.

At dawn on July 3rd, the Union left wing led the general assault, followed by the right wing and center, in one of the shortest major battles of the Civil War. The Union soldiers well knew what their generals chose to ignore. They pinned strips of paper to the back of their uniforms, on which their names and addresses had been written, to help identification of the corpses.

Despite inconsequential gains, the attack was an abysmal failure. In two hours Grant had lost 8,000 men to the Confederates 1,000. When he received orders to renew the assault, Smith, whose corps had been decimated, called the battle "a wanton waste of life." At noon, Grant appeared at Meade's headquarters to halt the attack.

Thousands of wounded lay on the battlefield, their pitiful cries plainly heard in the opposing trenches. Grant refused to request a ceasefire to collect the wounded, since it is the defeated party that usually asks for the truce. Two days later, Grant finally requested a two hour ceasefire, but by that time, hundreds of wounded had died from heat and thirst.

Rawlins had been in bitter opposition to a direct attack on the entrenched position. He told Wilson:

> The policy of direct and continuous attack, if persisted in, would ultimately so decimate and discourage the rank and file that they could not be induced to face the enemy at all.[370]

He blamed Grant's willingness to assail the fortified entrenchments at Cold Harbor on the murderous advice given by "Smash 'em up" Colonel C. B. Comstock, the regular army staff officer; and Dana agreed with Rawlins. Rawlins, however, completely misjudged the enemy casualties, believing them to be equal to those of the Union Army.[371]

Rawlins began to feel somewhat uncomfortable in this new and formal atmosphere. He was no longer the linchpin of former days.[372] On the other hand, he continued to maintain the friendliest of relations with General Meade, noting that:

> ...he [Meade] is of all men in the Army of the Potomac the one best fitted to command it. The opinion is not mine only, but is one frequently expressed by General Grant.[373]

Cold Harbor was the last of General Grant's direct attacks.[374] The overland campaign had advanced sixty miles at a cost of 60,000 casualties.[375] Thus ended seven of the bloodiest weeks of fighting on the American Continent. Neither the Union Army nor the country would countenance further frontal attacks on entrenched positions. Hospitals in and around Washington were overflowing. Fortunately, the erratic medical facilities of the first two years of the war had been replaced by twenty-five large hospitals in and around Washington, which struggled to keep abreast of the inflow of the wounded.

Following the debacle at Cold Harbor, Grant decided to abandon the Richmond front and move his army to Petersburg. Preparations were made for the Army of the Potomac to march southeast for forty miles, cross the James River over a 700-yard pontoon bridge and move on Petersburg, only twenty miles south of Richmond. The surprise march was made possible by a miscalculation of Lee. At the conclusion of the Cold Harbor battle, Lee had sent his cavalry to the Shenandoah, thus depriving his army of precious reconnaissance. He believed that Grant would attempt another flanking movement and was appalled to suddenly learn that Union forces had reached Petersburg. Only by a narrowest of margins had Lee been able to avert a Confederate disaster.

Most enemy supplies destined for the military and civilian populations enter Petersburg by rail and are forwarded by rail to Richmond. If Petersburg were to fall, Richmond would inevitably suffer a similar fate. Of the four rail lines entering Petersburg, two could easily be captured. The remaining two were the Weldon Railroad, coming from Wilmington, North Carolina, and the Southside Railroad, coming from the huge supply depot at Lynchburg, Virginia, one hundred miles west of Petersburg, and indirectly connected to the rich granaries of the Shenandoah Valley.

Before beginning the march to Petersburg on June 13, 1864, Grant returned Baldy Smith and his corps by night boat to Bermuda Hundred. From there, Smith was ordered to seize and occupy Petersburg, a day's march away.

At the time, the Petersburg trenches were thinly manned by only 2,000 Confederates. Smith had little difficulty in capturing a mile of the Petersburg entrenchments on June 15th, but instead of boldly entering the town, he waited for reinforcements. His troops were exhausted and demoralized after their depressing losses at Cold Harbor. Three additional Union corps arrived at Petersburg the next day. Union sorties were made on June 17th and the 18th, but before a concerted assault could be launched, the first of Lee's troops arrived after a fifty mile march; and barred entry into the city.

Rawlins noted that the one bright note in all the gloomy reports he received was the exploits of Smith's black troops, whom Rawlins praised:

> They did nobly and are entitled to be regarded as among the best of soldiers.[376]

Thus began the investment of Petersburg which would continue for nearly ten months, from mid-June, 1864 to April 1, 1865. It would not be a classic siege, not even a close investment, since the enemy could still draw supplies. Grant's intention now was to cut off the supplies entering the city, so that the enemy would be compelled to surrender or to be rendered so weak that a general assault would then be possible.

The news from the Shenandoah was disturbing. Lee had exploited the Cold Harbor victory to send Jubal Early into the Shenandoah, hoping to repeat the Confederate success with Stonewall Jackson in 1862. Early helped defeat Hunter at Lynchburg, and, after eluding Sigel, he slipped into Maryland. On July 9, 1864, he stunned the Northern public by audaciously exacting a ransom of $200,000, in return for sparing the town of Frederick, Maryland.

Rawlins wrote on June 17th from their new headquarters at City Point on the James River:

> …my health is improving and you may be assured no one seems less likely to be a subject of consumption than I.[377]

On June 20th he again wrote to Emma, instructing her to change greenbacks into gold. "Don't say to anyone I have advised you thus." The federal government had printed $450,000,000 in greenbacks, which became legal tender. From a value of ninety-seven cents in 1862, a greenback had plummeted to thirty-five cents by July 1864.[378] As the value of greenbacks declined, the price of gold rose. On June 24th, he wrote Emma that he, too, had converted $500 in greenbacks into gold.[379]

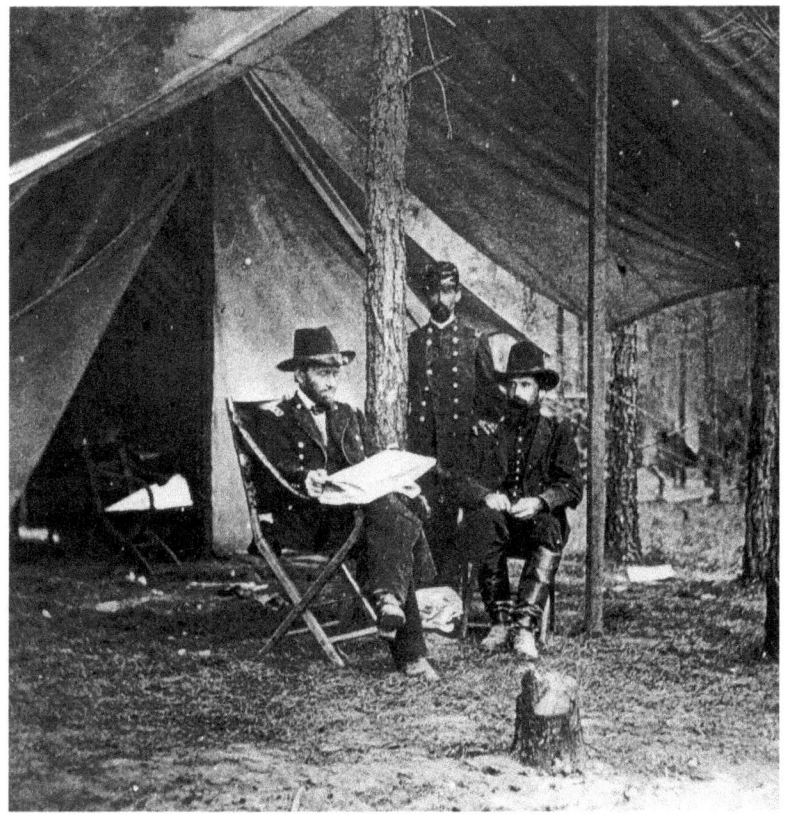

Grant, Badeau and Rawlins
Library of Congress

The enemy had an impressive system of entrenchments. First constructed in 1862, they extended east of Richmond, across the James, the Bermuda Hundred, the Appomattox and east and south of Petersburg, pointing to the west. The Union army quickly matched the enemy constructions with trenches, forts, redans and eventually retro-entrenchments, to prevent a surprise attack from the rear. Both sides brought in heavy cannon, trench mortars and the other engines of war then available. For the remainder of the war, the Army of the Potomac abstained from a direct attack on the enemy line, apart from the ill-fated mine explosion, shortly to be discussed, and the final assault at war's end when the Confederate line was being evacuated.

Henceforth, the goal of the Union Army would be to drive southwest in an effort to outflank the rebel entrenchment, or to reach and destroy the rails and roads supplying Petersburg. The three great conduits of enemy supply were the Weldon Railroad, the Southside Railroad and the Boydton Plank Road. The Jerusalem Plank Road to the east was used more for troop movement than for supply, since incoming wagons were vulnerable to Union attack.

Rawlins wrote Emma that he had urged Grant to enlist the help of the Speaker of the House of Representatives to defeat the $300 exemption clause in the draft law, which he passionately opposed on moral grounds.[380] Lincoln had recently issued a call for 300,000 volunteers for nine months service. If a governor could not deliver his quota of volunteers, a special draft was instituted to supply the deficit.[381] Any draftee chosen by lottery could purchase an exemption until the next drawing, upon payment of $300. If a man provided a substitute (usually at a cost of around $1,000) he would be exempt for the remainder of the war. Volunteers were paid an enlistment bounty of $600, and if they reenlisted they received an additional $100.

Summer should have been prime campaign time. Instead, the strength of the Army of the Potomac was at its lowest ebb. Sickness, wounds, desertion and the expiration of enlistments had all taken their toll.

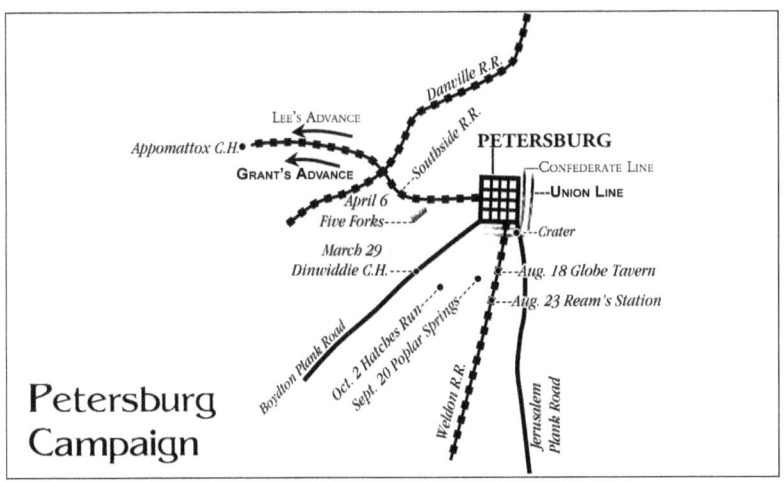

In June, Grant began driving to the southwest in an effort to cut supply lines or outflank the enemy. On June 22nd he had two corps probe the Jerusalem Plank Road, an auxiliary road into the city, but they were stopped by the hastily assembled Confederate forces. At the same time, two Union cavalry divisions were sent fifteen miles on a wide end run to the Southside Railroad, where they destroyed twenty-six miles of track. The damage was quickly repaired. On the way back to Union lines, the cavalry sustained heavy casualties.

On June 29th Rawlins wrote that Grant had been drinking on one of his inspection tours, when, for the first time, Rawlins had not been with him. "I shall hereafter under no circumstances fail to accompany him…"[382]

The oppressive summer heat was taking its toll, causing illness among the staff. Rawlins wrote on July 2nd[383] that Colonel Rowley's health was poor, and that he talked of resigning. Colonels Dent, Bowers and Duff were also in poor heath; and Colonel Babcock was ill in camp. "I am in very excellent health," he wrote. "My cough, although it still hangs on, is very slight indeed." To control the cough, Rawlins resorted to a mixture of old bourbon and cod liver oil.[384] He urged the other members of the staff to take whatever medical leave was required. After they had returned, he, too, would take a few days of leave. Later, he wrote that he could not leave, but did not disclose the reason.

From June on, the dullness of investment life was enlivened by reports of Sherman's progress as he advanced towards Atlanta, with General Joe Johnston fighting a delaying action. Johnston repeatedly intercepted the advancing Union Army, entrenched and waited for Sherman to attack. Sherman avoided direct assaults on entrenched positions, and instead, attempted to outflank Johnston; whereupon Johnston would retreat and repeat the maneuver. On June 27th, Sherman tried a direct assault on a fortified rebel position on Kenesaw Mountain, twenty miles north of Atlanta. He carried his objective but lost 3,000 men to the enemy's 450.

The Shenandoah never ceased to be a concern to Washington and an irritant to Grant, especially since there were relatively so few Rebel soldiers involved in the campaign. In the second week of July, Jubal Early crossed the Potomac and advanced on Washington. He easily brushed aside the hastily assembled Union troops at Monocacy River and reached Silver Springs, Maryland, on the outskirts of Washington. By July 11th Early was in position to threaten the Capital. How far he would have pursued his attack is a matter for conjecture. Washington had thirty-seven miles of entrenchments and sixty-four forts; but it also had a population that frightened easily.

Dana wrote a blistering letter to Rawlins criticizing Grant for previously stripping Washington of its troops.[385] At Lincoln's frantic request, an army corps was rushed by train to Washington to man the defenses.[386] Its timely appearance persuaded Early to withdraw, if indeed he had other intentions. Its mission accomplished, the Union corps was returned to Petersburg.

Early continued his rampage, ravaging Maryland and burning Chambersburg. A perturbed Lincoln requested that Grant report to him in Washington. Rawlins insisted that Grant's place was in Petersburg and that his appearance in Washington might be misinterpreted as a change in tactics.[387] Heeding his advice, Grant planned to send Rawlins to placate the president.

By July, the Baldy Smith situation came to a boil. Smith, who had been sent to stiffen the resolve of the Army of the James, had proven to be cantankerous and disruptive. Moreover, he had been wildly indiscreet in his criticisms of Butler, Meade, and Grant himself. On July 19th, Grant relieved him of command of his corps and appointed General E. O. Ord in his place.

Once relieved, Smith let fly charges of Grant's drunkenness, artfully corroborated by the testimony of another officer. Smith stated that in early July, when Butler had taken Grant on a tour of the corps headquarters, Butler arranged that Grant be given an alcoholic drink at each stop, etc. By the time the tour ended, Grant was thoroughly intoxicated.[388] When informed of the incident,[389] Rawlins is supposed to have said. "There's the general drunk again after all those promises I got from the corps commanders." Rawlins later confronted Butler, who stated that he had seen Grant drink wine and nothing else. To Senator Hoar, however, Butler stated that he could prove Grant was drunk on seven occasions.[390] Curiously, Rawlins makes no mention of this episode in his frank letter to Emma on July 19th,[391] so it is possible that the story may (or may not) have been contrived, in whole or in part. At any rate, nine days later Rawlins was confronted by another instance of Grant's drinking.[392]

By July 20th, the Atlanta campaign was showing progress. Sherman had been maneuvering skillfully, but continued to rely on the railroad for supplies. Johnston had fallen back to the Chattahoochee River, six miles from Atlanta and had begun to entrench. Ahead loomed the gloomy prospect of another siege, which dismayed the Northern public. The one siege at Petersburg was more than sufficient.

The president of the Confederate States, Jefferson Davis, by this time, was bone-weary of Johnston's retreats. He relieved Johnston on July 17th, appointing in his place General John Bell Hood. Hood, who had lost a leg at Chickamauga and the use of an arm at Gettysburg, was a born brawler, committed to a vigorous defense of Atlanta, but even he recognized that his army was weak and exhausted.

On July 23rd, the staff was plunged into mourning, with the news of the death of General James B. McPherson, shot outside of Atlanta. His horse is said to have returned to headquarters with an empty saddle. Grant cried when he heard the news. The fearless McPherson had been a particular favorite of Rawlins, who lamented:

> My friend, with whom I have shared the same blanket, messed at the same board, endured the fatigue of the march, the exposure of the storm and faced the dangers of battle.[393]

Sherman attacked east and west of Atlanta, then struck south of the city, seizing Eastport, a vital railroad terminal. Union siege guns were brought in to shell the center. On September 2nd, Hood abandoned Atlanta, and the Union forces entered the city. To Lincoln, who had grave concerns about the outcome of the forthcoming presidential election in November, the news came as manna from heaven.

At the end of July, two probing attacks were made north of Petersburg, with no gains. The Confederate position appeared secure, and the two Petersburg railroads supplying Petersburg were running smoothly.

Rawlins visited Washington July 25th, carrying dispatches for the president and the secretary of war. He answered questions and listened to complaints, especially about the Shenandoah. He remained in the city for two days, while he implemented Grant's plans to unify the various commands around Washington. The goal was to curtail enemy activities in the Shenandoah with the minimum of Union troops. In this way, Union strength at Petersburg would not be depleted.

In Washington, Dana's opinion of Rawlins had grown in the past twelve months:

> Public servants of his quality will always be few. There are plenty of men whose name will flourish in history without having rendered a tithe of his unostentatious and invaluable contributions to the great work of the nation.[394]

When he returned to City Point, Rawlins was disappointed to discover that Grant had again been drinking. He told Emma:

> I find the General in my absence digressed from his true path.

He added in desperation:

> The God of Heaven only knows how long I am to serve my country as the guardian of the habits of him who it has honored…Owing to this faltering, I shall not be able to leave here till the rebel movement in Maryland is settled and also the fate of Atlanta.[395]

Notwithstanding his fears, he left for Danbury on June 25th.

Meanwhile, another opportunity had been missed. The soldiers of the 48th Pennsylvania, coal miners in civilian life, had begun, in late June, the construction of a 500-foot tunnel under the enemy line. On July 30th at five a.m., after a month of labor, they exploded four tons of explosive. The blast blew an enormous crater 170 feet wide and 600 feet long. Instead of skirting the crater, the Union soldiers charged into it and were trapped by its thirty foot walls. In all, the Union had sustained 4,000 casualties.

Grant had left the details of this major assault to Meade, who had left it to Burnside, and he, in turn, to the division commander. No one, not even Lee, who must have known of the mining,[396] had confidence in the success of the venture, and this doubt had been communicated down the line. Both Grant and Meade had been kept informed of the progress, as had Rawlins, who had left on leave five days before the explosion. The tunnel was a dismal failure, for which Grant bore the ultimate responsibility. Secretary of War Stanton was especially incensed that the lives of a thousand black soldiers had been recklessly thrown away. General Ambrose Burnside was given no meaningful assignment for the rest of the war.

Grant by now had had his fill of Jubal Early and the Shenandoah. To add to the public concern in the

North, Early had sent cavalry to rampage Pennsylvania, and on July 30th the Confederate soldiers set fire to Chambersburg, in retaliation for the Federal vandalism in the Valley.

Grant was determined to end the menace of Jubal Early by sending Sheridan into the Shenandoah. "I want Sheridan...to put himself south of the enemy and follow him [Early] to the death," wrote Grant. Sheridan arrived in early August to assume his first independent command. Grant had merged four departments into the one Middle Military Department.[397]

To discourage Lee from sending reinforcements to Early, Grant maintained pressure on the Petersburg line. Sheridan got off to a slow start. For five weeks Sheridan ranged the countryside, burning farms and carrying off livestock, but failed to force a confrontation with the enemy.

The coming of the hot weather permitted Rawlins to take a few weeks of sick leave, subject to recall in case of an emergency. Bowers kept Rawlins informed by letter about even the most mundane matters. He reported that he had denied the headquarters sutler a permit to sell liquor. When the Quartermaster threatened to take the matter up with Rawlins on his return, Bowers assured him that Rawlins would concur with his decision. In early

August, a Confederate operative exploded a time bomb aboard an ammunition barge docked at City Point. Forty men were killed and many injured, among them Colonel Orville E. Babcock, when a bomb fragment struck headquarters. Thereafter, the staff redoubled its efforts to guard the General.[398] Parker kept a loaded revolver ready at all times.[399]

There had been staff changes in August. Rowley resigned because of ill health and returned to Galena. Then Bowers was called away by family illness, and the task of keeping Rawlins informed temporarily fell to Captain George K. Leet, AAG. Parker, who had the best handwriting of the staff,[400] replaced Bowers as "private secretary" and was promoted to lieutenant colonel. This pleased the Galena crowd, since there was estrangement between the old and the new staff members. "We have the hardest kind of work to get along with the new people," Parker wrote.[401]

Among his many tasks, Parker managed Grant's correspondence. While at work, he often sat at Grant's desk. One day, a visitor who had met Grant in Cairo was shown the tent. When he saw Parker, he remarked, "Well, that's him, but he's got all fired sun-burned since I last had a look at him."[402]

By the end of August, the Army of the Potomac had been reduced to no more than 44,000 effectives,[403] including a considerable number of support troops. Also, the quality of the corps had significantly deteriorated, with the influx of the new replacements. To add to Grant's concern, Halleck informed him that the ninety-day enlistments were about to expire. These were men who had been engaged in guard duty at prisons and depots, but their replacements would have to come from Grant's command. Finally, the Army of the Potomac might be required to send troops to the northern cities to quell civil disturbances resulting from the draft. These shortages were sure to limit Union initiatives.

Despite the reduction in the numbers of the Union troops and their enervation by the heat, Grant kept probing to the southwest. On August 18th an infantry corps finally captured the Globe Tavern Station on the Weldon Railroad, four miles south of Petersburg. Trenches were hastily dug and connected to the Union line. The enemy compensated by diverting supplies from the Weldon Railroad to the Boydton Plank Road, which led to Petersburg. On August 25th another corps was ordered to destroy additional track, but it was repulsed at Reame's Station farther up the Weldon line.

After Bowers had returned to duty on August 25th, he reported to Rawlins:

> I regret to say that Grant has been quite unwell for the past ten days. He feels languid and feeble and is hardly able to keep about, yet he tends to business

promptly and his daily walk and conduct are unexceptional.[404]

Grant had also been troubled with episodes of gastrointestinal distress and bouts of migraine which recurred every three to four weeks.[405] True migraine is among the most painful of human afflictions.

Grant tried every reasonable expedient to gain advantage.[406] As the siege entered its fourth month, Grant again probed north of the James. Despite some initial successes, the Union troops were beaten back.

Action was desultory in September, pending the arrival of replacements. Since no immediate action was planned, Grant insisted that Rawlins prolong his leave. Grant was no stranger to pulmonary sickness. His own brother, Simpson, had died of consumption. On September 25th Babcock advised Rawlins to give up field duty and set up his headquarters in Washington. His advice fell on deaf ears.

At the end of September, while Lee was fending off the Union thrusts north of the James River, Grant again sent Union troops to the southwest toward the Boydton Plank Road. A Confederate corps opposed them at Peebles Farm, two miles east of the Weldon line, and forced the Union troops to retreat. Even so, the Union Army could further extend their line an additional three miles, and they build an anchoring fort.

Lee, too, was compelled to extend his line, to protect his road and railroad supply lines. He now had thirty miles of Petersburg entrenchments to maintain. Notwithstanding, Grant was unable to slip by the Confederate line. He began to believe that this state of affairs might continue until Sheridan returned and brought with him sufficient cavalry to outflank the Confederate position.

After three months in Danbury, Rawlins left for Petersburg. Dana saw him in Washington and noted "signs of increasing disease." Grant shook his head and murmured to the staff, "I do not like that cough."[407] But to Julia, Grant wrote:

Rawlins appears to have entirely recovered.[408]

Arriving in City Point, Rawlins reassured Emma:

I find here every convenience for my comfort.[409]

A large town had spring up at City Point, on the south embankment of the James. Shacks, cottages, sheds, log huts and tents were now arranged into streets, swarming with military personnel, newspapermen, clerks and foreign observers. Bakeries, warehouses, hospitals, sutlers' tents and baseball fields were everywhere; and a railroad line now skirted the trenches. The Union supply depots were capable of feeding 100,000 men and 300,000 mounts (if they had them), while the Confederate soldiers often went unfed for days.

Arrangements were made to spare Rawlins the petty details of daily staff work. Lieutenant William McKee Dunn, Jr., was assigned to him as AAG. Rawlins had arrived at a critical moment. With the public impatient for progress, some military leaders were now urging a direct assault on the Confederate line. Rawlins vigorously opposed this action and insisted that the "siege" be continued.[410] He pleaded with the War Department for reinforcements, especially troops not actively employed elsewhere. His pleas were heeded. Reinforcements were beginning to arrive—on some days as many as a thousand men.

The failure to end the siege had been very distressing to Lincoln, but he continued to support Grant:

> Hold on with a bulldog grip and chew and choke as much as possible.[411]

In early October 1864, Rawlins and Parker visited General Butler, with whom Rawlins had maintained cordial relations, although critical of his performance. It is likely Butler told Rawlins what he later wrote in 1892, that it was Smith and not he, who had earlier given the whiskey to Grant during that fateful visit in July.[412]

Sheridan was still maneuvering cautiously in the Shenandoah. With the election only two months away, the president was desperate to see results. Grant, too, was impatient. He traveled by rail to meet Sheridan and to press him for action. On September 19, 1864, Sheridan won a hard fought victory over Early at Winchester, Virginia; and again, three days later, at Fisher Hill. Then a month went by while the enemy recuperated and gathered strength. On October 19th, Early suddenly attacked at dawn the Union encampment at Cedar Creek, Virginia, and for a while seemed to have prevailed.

Although twenty miles from the battle, Sheridan sped to the scene on horseback, rallied the Union horse soldiers and converted defeat into victory. Sheridan was made a major general in the regular army, and the name of "Rienzi," his horse, passed into history. In short order, the Union army severed the Virginia Central Railroad and other lines into Richmond. Barns were burned, crops destroyed, bridges razed, and fruit trees girded.[413] Although still at large, Early was no longer a serious threat.

On October 27th, another compound Union maneuver was attempted. Three Union corps moving somewhat parallel to each other drove toward Burgess Mill, a mile from the Boydton Plank Road, intending from there to drive towards the Southside

Railroad. The inner corps closest to Petersburg was promptly stalled. The middle corps reached the Boydton Plank Road but was confronted by enemy troops rushed there from Petersburg. The outer corps failed to push forward. The Union troops withdrew without any addition made to their entrenchments.

In the absence of progress on the Petersburg front, Sherman continued to hold the public interest. An astonishing report appeared in the Confederate newspapers that Hood, having abandoned Atlanta, was now moving *north!* According to the Confederate newspapers, his intention was to cut Sherman's supply line and retake Nashville and Tennessee, all of which would compel the Union Army to abandon Atlanta and to turn north to engage him. On October 10th Rawlins wrote, "this movement was unexpected, and makes even Grant scratch his head."[414]

What action should Sherman next take? Should he pursue Hood's army and defeat it, before setting out for the Atlantic Ocean or the Gulf? This is what Rawlins advised,[415] and Grant tended to agree.[416] If Hood were left unchecked, he could devastate Tennessee and Kentucky and undo all that the Union Army had accomplished in the past two years. If he were to reach the Ohio River, the news would ruin Lincoln's chances in the coming election, thereby achieving a long-sought Confederate goal. Rawlins had earlier written on October 15th:

> It may be that Sherman has cut loose and gone down through Georgia, but I think not. Too fine an opportunity presents itself for the entire destruction of Hood's army for Sherman not to avail himself of it...[417]

And still hopeful that Sherman would delay his departure, Rawlins wrote that *after* Hood's defeat:

> Why you may look for Sherman within a few weeks to come out at some one of the great Atlantic or Gulf cities.[418]

The matter was argued in camp long into the night, some for the march, Rawlins against it—at least until Hood had been defeated. Porter says of Rawlins:

> Rawlins talked with great force. He had a natural taste for public speaking and when he became particularly earnest in the discussion of a question, his speech often took the form of an oration and, as he grew more excited, he would hold forth in stentorian tones and emphasize his remarks with vehement gesticulations and no end of expletives.[419]

On one occasion, Grant came into the tent at one a.m. while a heated discussion was still in progress. "Go to bed, all of you!" he snapped. "You're keeping the whole camp awake!"[420]

There is no evidence that Rawlins ever discussed the matter surreptitiously with Washington, although on one occasion, as will be seen, Rawlins and Stanton did journey together by boat from City Point to Washington. Both Stanton and Lincoln were deeply troubled by Sherman's proposed "March to the Sea," while Hood was still afoot. Grant, too, had his doubts, but eventually deferred to Sherman's judgment.

As to the charge that Rawlins maneuvered behind Grant's back, Cadwallader writes:

> Rawlins had no concealment as Chief of Staff. General Grant might sometimes attempt some minor concealment from Rawlins, not affecting public or official duties, but it was not in the nature of the latter to do so. Scores of cases can be cited in which Rawlins took strong pronounced ground against complicated operations; but not one in which he concealed his opposition.[421]

Sherman was a good friend of Rawlins, about whom Rawlins wrote:

> May prudence prosper and preserve him is my earnest prayer.[422]

Notwithstanding, in his 1885 memoirs Grant writes:

> I was in favor of Sherman's plan from the time it was first submitted to me. My Chief of Staff was bitterly opposed to it and as I learned subsequently, finding

that he could not move me, he appealed to the authorities at Washington to stop it.[423]

This statement created a furor among Grant's friends. Cadwallader, who was with the staff at the time, emphatically denied that Rawlins ever appealed to the War Department to put a stop to Sherman.[424] Although Sherman supported Grant's assertion,[425] he later had some reservations, when he wrote to a friend:

> ...what can you or I or anybody say [about the Rawlins affair] after the publication of Grant's Memoirs?[426]

In the end, Sherman was allowed to rely on his own judgment, rather than on that of the War Department. "Councils of war do not fight," Grant said.[427] Sherman detached George Thomas and his army from his command and sent them north to engage Hood, but he gave them worn-out horses and the weaker infantry units. Sherman accompanied Thomas almost halfway to Nashville and together they made a spirited attempt to corner Hood, and failed. This unsuccessful attempt to engage Hood demonstrated the futility of chasing a rebel army determined to evade battle.[428] Meanwhile, a golden opportunity would have been lost by not marching towards the sea.

On November 2nd, Grant wired Sherman:

Go, as you propose.[429]

The closure of Mobile Bay (August 23rd), the fall of Atlanta (September 3rd), and the victory at Cedar Creek (October 18th) all had a determinate effect on the presidential election. Lincoln was reelected in November 1864 with a popular majority of 400,000 votes and an Electoral College margin of 212 to twenty-one. The vote confirmed a renewed public support for the war.[430]

Sherman and his army set out from Atlanta on November 19th on an 800-mile trek to Savannah. They marched in two columns in a sixty-mile swath and foraged off the land. "I can make this march and make Georgia howl" Sherman had written. His men burned and destroyed $100 million in property, and Georgia did, indeed, weep.

Hood, meanwhile, had moved north toward Nashville, with Thomas' army following close on his heels. Reinforcements for Thomas' army were desperately needed, if there was to be any hope of stopping Hood.

An urgent request for reinforcements was dispatched to Rosencrans in St. Louis, who was expected to furnish the largest share of the needed troops. When the soldiers were not forthcoming, Grant asked that Rosencrans be replaced; but Halleck demurred.[431]

Rawlins wrote reassuring letters to Emma:

> I am ten pounds heavier than my usual weight which is 155 pounds.[432]

Two days later:

> I have no doubt of my recovery.

J. Russell Jones, now turned patron of the arts, arranged to have the painter, John Antrobus, make a portrait of Rawlins, as he had done for Grant. The portrait shows a sorely debilitated man.[433]

In view of the urgent needs of Thomas' army, Grant ordered Rawlins to go to St. Louis, to hasten the delivery of the reinforcements. Rawlins left by boat to Washington, accompanied by Halleck, who had been on a visit to City Point; and then, unaccompanied, Rawlins journeyed by train to St. Louis. During a free moment, he paid a courtesy visit to Julia Grant at her father's home. Julia sent her regards to Emma and asked that Emma join her for a visit to City Point.

Although Rosencrans received Rawlins cordially, he was hesitant to deplete his command. At the time, the Union's hold on Missouri was tenuous. Rosencrans was fearful of the secret societies, the civil unrest and the growing strength of Sterling Price, the irrepressible Confederate general.[434] Rawlins could not hope to allay his fears but argued that the loss of St. Louis was not of primary concern, since the outcome of the war would be determined by events elsewhere.[435]

Rawlins sent Thomas every available soldier that he could raise, altogether some 14,000 men.[436] As always, Rawlins' faith was more "in the infallibility of numbers than in the infallibility of generals." Despite his best efforts, weeks passed before the reinforcements reached Thomas, and many did not arrive until the very last moment. Meanwhile, Rawlins continued to be troubled by Hood's campaign. He sensed that Hood's plans had great merit; and that if Hood were to fail, it would only be because he had delayed his departure from Atlanta.[437]

After completing his assignment in St. Louis, Rawlins stopped briefly in Danbury and Washington and arrived at City Point on November 15th. The next day, Grant, accompanied by Comstock and Badeau, left for a week's visit to his wife and children in Burlington, New Jersey, leaving the war in Rawlins' hands. "I hope he will keep all straight during his absence," wrote Rawlins.[438] With Grant away, Rawlins became the acting general-in-chief of the U.S. Army and sent orders under his own signature.[439]

Grant returned nine days later. Meanwhile, the country was anxiously awaiting news from Thomas. Hood's army advanced towards Nashville, but the road was blocked by a hastily entrenched Union corps (Schofield) at a town called "Franklin," fifteen miles from Nashville. Hood attacked on November 30th, without the benefit of artillery preparation, and lost a quarter of his men and thirteen generals. Although he had suffered a major set-back, Hood was still determined to take Nashville.

On the Petersburg front, an attempt was made on December 8th to tear up additional track of the Weldon Railroad. A corps was sent south along the Jerusalem Plank Road to a point sixteen miles south of Petersburg and then west to the Weldon rail line. Approximately forty miles of track was destroyed, but the arrival of Confederate forces and the onset of inclement weather halted further progress.

Two weeks passed since the Battle of Franklin, and Thomas still awaited reinforcements. Brigadier General James Wilson was sent from Virginia to offer assistance, but his command was in sore need of remounting. Still lacking cavalry, Thomas collected horses from farmers, streetcar companies and even circuses.[440] Meanwhile, the country demanded action, and an impatient Washington urged Grant to replace "Slow Trot" Thomas. Both Lincoln and Grant showered him with dispatches. Finally, Grant ordered General John Logan to relieve Thomas, and Grant, himself, set out for Nashville. At the last moment, the reinforcements from Missouri arrived in Nashville.

While Grant was in transit, the news reached him that on December 16th Thomas had defeated Hood in a stunning victory outside of Nashville. Some call it the most decisive battle of the Civil War.[441] Thereafter, Hood's army all but disintegrated. After the excitement subsided, Grant summoned a large part of Thomas' troops to Virginia for the forthcoming spring offensive. He sent Wilson's cavalry south in a spectacular raid into Alabama and Georgia.

More astonishing news came from Georgia on Christmas Day. *Sherman Had Taken Savannah!* The nation was delirious with excitement. Initially, Grant planned to have Sherman establish a base on the Atlantic coast and then move his troops by ship from Savannah to City Point, where they would join the Army of the Potomac. Rawlins disagreed vehemently with this proposal, but further argument ended, when it was discovered that the Union lacked sufficient shipping to transport the Union troops. Instead, Sherman would have the privilege of marching north, to give South Carolina "a real taste of the war."[442]

Christmas Eve was a dull place at City Point. Cadwallader wandered into Colonel Bowers' tent to chat. Then Rawlins entered and reminded them that taps had sounded. Five minutes later Grant wandered in and opened a box of cigars.[443]

In January 1865, the capture of Fort Fisher buoyed up Union hopes. This almost impregnable fort guarded Wilmington, North Carolina, the last key port open to blockade runners. General Butler had brought up troops in December, but after a feeble attempt to capture the fort, he withdrew, much to the disgust of Admiral David Porter, the naval commander. On January 15th, General Alfred Terry, a lawyer in civilian life, launched a skillful assault on Fort Fisher, with naval assistance, and succeeded in capturing it. This triumph closed off the last remaining seaport of the Confederacy. No longer could the Weldon Railroad carry weapons or supplies from abroad.

With the presidential election now past, the time had come for General Benjamin Butler to depart the scene. His pathetic performance at Fort Fisher was the final indignity. Cadwallader had long distrusted Butler and had often spoken disparagingly of him to Rawlins within Grant's earshot.[444] On January 4, 1865 Grant formally requested Butler's removal. Butler still maintained friendly relations with Rawlins and wrote him that he attributed his dismissal to the hostility of the other members of Grant's staff.[445]

Rawlins, Emma and Jennie at City Point
Library of Congress

In January, Julia and Jesse visited City Point and were lodged in a three-room log and board cottage. With them came Emma and Rawlins' daughter, Jennie. Rawlins had earlier questioned the propriety of having a conjugal visit, when field officers were denied this privilege.[446] He also had concern for the care for his other two youngsters, while Emma was away; but allowed Emma to make the decision.[447] In the end, Emma and Jennie came to City Point and remained until the closing days of the war, lodged in a converted storehouse.

The winter was cold and it rained often. Colonels Porter and Badeau went on sick leave; Grant suffered from a digestive disorder. Yet, Grant insisted that his army be ready to march.[448]

Probing to the southwest continued. On February 5th two corps were sent to Boydton Plank Road to capture wagons transporting enemy supplies from a transfer point on the Weldon Railroad. Union intelligence had overestimated the supply column, since only eighteen wagons were captured. The Federal troops were halted at Hatcher's Run, four miles east of the Boydton Plank Road, but Federal trenches could be further extended. Lee now had thirty-five miles of Petersburg entrenchments to actively maintain and an additional fifteen miles east of the city, with barely 1,000 men for each mile of trench.[449]

By February 16, 1865 Sherman had reached Columbia, South Carolina, and watched the flames consume the city.

Also of note was the arrival of Captain Robert Lincoln, son of the president, who joined Grant's staff as a junior ADC, and was assigned the duty of conducting visitors. He remained until war's end. Prior to this, he had been following the war from the comforts of Harvard, but was now anxious the add luster to his résumé. In fairness to Robert, his mother previously had forbidden him to join the army.

Congress, under Washburne's leadership, had created the permanent office of chief of staff and with it, the rank of brigadier general, USA. On March 3, 1865 the appointment was tendered to John A. Rawlins, the last generalship in the regular army created during the Civil War.[450]

Sheridan brought his mission in the Shenandoah to a close in March 1865, with the destruction of the Shenandoah railroads supplying Richmond. He was ordered to cut the rail line between Petersburg and Richmond, but could not complete this assignment, since he lacked pontoon boats with which to cross the James River. Sheridan remounted, refitted, and on March 27th rejoined the Army of the Potomac.

Initially, Grant had planned to send Sheridan to assist Sherman in the proposed march north to Petersburg. Rawlins disagreed with this arrangement and insisted that Sheridan remain at Petersburg, to which Grant reluctantly agreed. Later, Grant would say that the plan to send Sheridan south was proposed only to deceive the enemy.[451] "Let's end the business *here!*" Grant muttered. Sheridan was given command not only of his own corps, but also of whatever infantry was needed to support his efforts to seize the South Side Railroad.

By now, the futility of holding the Confederate trenches around Petersburg was apparent to General Lee. The Union Army kept extending its line, and the Confederates were barely able to keep apace, their numbers shrinking daily from illness and desertion. Lee began preparations to abandon the Richmond-Petersburg trenches and to move is troops south to join General Joseph Johnston, whose army was now confronting Sherman's troops.

Before doing so, Lee had to disengage his army from the entrenchments. He ordered an assault on the Union's Fort Stedman, a mile from Meade's headquarters, in the hope that Grant would pour in troops to seal off the breech, thereby permitting Lee's army to slip away. The assault was made on a part of the line held by a single Union corps. Although initially successful, the Confederate attack on March 25th was contained after a few hours of fighting with a loss of 4,000 Confederate casualties.

Grant thinned his line around the Bermuda Hundred and moved the troops to the southwest. He ordered a renewed attack on the Confederate right flank, in what today would be called a wide end run (cavalry) with several rows of blockers (infantry).

The total Confederate line by now was fifty-three miles long.[452]

On March 27th-28th he ordered one corps to cross the Weldon Railroad and attack the Confederate line. To the south, he positioned two tiers of infantry corps, all in light marching order, as well as Sheridan's cavalry corps. The two infantry corps began driving west. The inner corps came to the Boydton Plank Road; the outer corps crossed it; and Sheridan, without hindrance, crossed it further south and advanced. For two days the Union troops drove without significant opposition. On the 31st of March the outermost infantry corps encountered strong Confederate resistance, and cut short the engagement at nightfall. Sheridan advanced to Five Forks, midway between the Boydton Plank Road and the Southside Railroad. Here he encountered a well-entrenched Confederate position and could make little progress. He bivouacked the night at nearby Dinwiddie Court House on the Boydton Plank Road.

The following morning, April 1st, Sheridan and his troops advanced toward Five Forks, a few miles from Southside Railroad. Torrential rain had turned the roads into a quagmire. The corps commander of the outer corps was ordered to come to his support. The outer infantry corps made a trying march through the mud and began an attack on the enemy flank. After a heated battle, the Confederate resistance at Five Forks collapsed.

There was great excitement at Union headquarters. Sensing real progress, Grant and his staff had left City Point and were following behind Sheridan. On April 2nd Grant ordered a general attack on the Confederate line by the other Union corps still occupying the trenches. With Lee evacuating troops from Petersburg defenses, the Confederate line was soon breeched in three places.

Sheridan had already reached the Southside Railroad and was preparing to follow the retreating Confederate army, when Rawlins brought up the matters of the stormy weather and the lack of fodder for Sheridan's horses.[453] A cavalry corps requires the support of one thousand wagons.[454] Sheridan insisted that he be allowed to vigorously pursue the fleeing Confederate army. "I'll get all the forage I want!" he exclaimed.[455] In his memoirs Grant writes that Rawlins had recommended that the cavalry return to City Point to resupply,[456] but this, once again, is not quite accurate. Because of the weather and scarcity of fodder, Grant himself had authorized a "retrograde movement,"[457] but as the rain subsided, all three concurred that Sheridan would advance and procure fodder along the way from a Union supply train, when it caught up to him.

General Lee had clearly foreseen that Sherman's arrival at Petersburg would have been an insurmountable difficulty. His objective now was to unite forces with General Johnston and defeat Sherman's army. Then, he would return with Johnston to Virginia to re-engage the Army of the Potomac. Lee began his retreat towards Lynchburg, Virginia, marching along the Richmond-Danville Railroad line to Amelia Court House, thirty miles west of Petersburg. The Union forces followed in a somewhat parallel route, along the Southside Rail line.

On April 4th Rawlins sent word to Emma to return to Danbury, since he would not be returning to City Point. A dispatch boat was readied to take Julia, Emma and the children to Washington; but they lingered.[458] Meanwhile Sheridan swept ahead, crossed the Southside Railroad tracks and spread out over the network of roads south of the Appomattox Court House.

Rawlins and Parker followed at Grant's side. Since Rowley had resigned in March because of bad health and Joe Bowers had been left behind at headquarters, the duties of the AAG fell once again on Rawlins.[459] Reports poured in ceaselessly and had to be sorted out. Supply was a constant worry.

After failing to obtain provisions at Amelia Court House, on the Danville line, Lee and his army abandoned the rail track and proceeded cross-country, following the Southside Railroad (which had crossed the Danville line). Midday, Union cavalry intercepted the Confederate Army at Sayler's Creek, and, after a vigorous attack, compelled the surrender of a third of Lee's army. The remainder proceeded toward Appomattox Court House Station, seventy-five miles west of Petersburg, where again they expected to find provisions. For three days Lee's Army marched without food and supplies, with the Union army dogging the flank and the rear of the Confederates. Finally, at Appomattox Court House, Lee found, instead of supplies, Sheridan's cavalry. *Checkmate!*

Grant wrote to General Lee on April 7th that events justify Grant asking for surrender. On the same day, Lee requested terms. Grant answered that since "peace" was his object, the enemy soldiers and officers were to be disqualified from taking up arms until properly exchanged, etc. To this Lee replied that he had no intention of surrendering his army, but "as far as your proposal may…lead to the restoration of peace, I shall be glad to meet you…"

The message was delivered to Rawlins, who read it aloud. Rawlins was infuriated. He immediately pointed out:

> He [Lee] wants to entrap us into making a treaty of peace. No, sir. *NO, SIR*!

Grant replied that "it amounts to the same thing. Lee is only trying to be let down easily."

"He has to *SURRENDER*!" Rawlins thundered." It shall be *SURRENDER*—and nothing else!"

Grant persisted: "If I meet Lee, he will surrender before I leave."

"You have no right to meet Lee or anybody else to arrange terms of peace!" Rawlins retorted: "That is the prerogative of the President and the Senate. Your business is to capture or destroy Lee's army!"

He reminded Grant that when a Confederate Peace Commission had come to City Point a few weeks before, Stanton became enraged and had written him:

> The President directs me to say to you that he wishes you to have no conference with General Lee unless it be for the capitulation of Lee's army…You are not to decide, discuss or confer upon any political question…[460]

Grant heeded the Rawlins objections and replied to Lee:

> As I have no authority to treat on the subject of peace, the meeting proposed by you...could lead to no good.

No one slept that night. Grant had an attack of agonizing migraine and spent the night with mustard plasters on his wrist and head, and his feet soaked in hot water. At eleven o'clock the next day as headquarters was en route to join Sheridan, a messenger delivered a letter. Rawlins read it and handed it to Grant, who asked that Rawlins read it aloud:

> 9 April 1865. General: I received your note of this morning [and seek to] ascertain definitely what terms were embraced...with reference to the surrender of this army. I now ask an interview in accordance with your letter of yesterday, for that purpose. R. E. Lee

Grant replied that he would meet Lee at any place he chose. He handed the note to Rawlins.

"How will that do, Rawlins?"

"I think *that* will do," Rawlins smiled.

After the surrender at Appomattox, Grant and Rawlins returned to City Point. The trip took two days and was made on hastily repaired rail lines. The train ran off its tracks three times.[461] Grant brought Julia and Emma and the children back to Washington. After lodging them in the Willard Hotel, he reported to the president.[462] The following day Julia, Emma and the two children ate a late lunch.

The Grants begged off an invitation to accompany the Lincolns to Ford's Theater that evening and instead left for Burlington, New Jersey, where their other children had been left in the care of Grant's sister.[463]

The war did not quite end with Lee's capitulation. Sherman was still in North Carolina, arranging terms of surrender with General Johnston. The terms first offered wildly exceeded Sherman's authority and were promptly repudiated by Secretary of War Stanton. The provisions had allowed the Confederates to keep their slaves, to elect state governments and to arrange for the settlement of Confederate debts. Stanton prevailed on Grant to intervene, which he did with great tact. The revised terms were similar to those offered by Grant and were accepted by Johnston. Elsewhere, hostilities in Alabama came to an end when Mobile was occupied by Union troops and when Jefferson Davis was captured by the Wilson expedition. Not until late June 1865 did the last rebel detachment in Texas lay down its arms.

Secretary of War Rawlins
Brady-Handy Collection, Library of Congress

FINAL DAYS

Of immediate concern at the end of the war was the presence of Emperor Maximilian in Mexico. Both Rawlins and Grant were deeply sympathetic to the Mexican cause and vigorously supported the secretary of war, when he ordered Sheridan's army of 50,000 Volunteers and Wilson's cavalry to the Mexican border. Grant even envisioned a military invasion by an army of Union and ex-Confederate soldiers, but the crisis subsided when the French army withdrew, and Emperor Maximilian was executed.[464]

On April 9th, Rawlins was brevetted with the rank of Major General USV "for gallant and meritorious service during the campaign terminating with the surrender of the insurgent army under Lee." Through some error, Rawlins' name initially had not been included in the lists to be brevetted, so Grant reminded Congress:

> No staff officer ever before had it in his power to render as much service and no one ever performed his duties more faithfully or efficiently.[465]

The cessation of hostilities left Rawlins, as Chief of Staff, with the monumental task of compiling and collating terminal reports and returns, in preparation for Grant's final report of operations. Thousands of claims, protests, demands and complaints were thrust at him for investigation. He was assisted in his work by Bowers, Parker and Leet. In the final report, Grant, as usual, prepared a brief outline, but left the details to Rawlins and his staff. The result was a remarkable record of the military proceedings of the Richmond and Petersburg campaign.

The Grand Review on May 24, 1865 had required several weeks of tedious preparation. Still, not everything went smoothly. Sherman was outraged that he had to learn the details of the parade from a newspaper.[466] Sheridan was away at the Mexican border with his troops.

Rawlins and Emma returned to the Hurlburt home on Franklin Street in Danbury and made preparations for a move to Washington. Grant and Julia toured the country, deeply immersed in receptions, parades and dinners, which they greatly enjoyed. Galena and Philadelphia each gave them a house; New York donated $100,000, and Boston contributed books, worth $5,000. In the Philadelphia home, Julia found a lavishly-stocked wine cellar. On the advice of Rawlins, she had the wine sold.[467] In July 1866,

Grant was made a four-star General of the Army. Tragically, Joe Bowers was killed in a train accident, returning with Grant from West Point. Parker replaced him as senior ADC.

Both Grant and Rawlins initially supported the undemanding Reconstruction policy of President Andrew Johnson, whose sole requirements were that the South renounce secession, recognize emancipation and repudiate the Confederate public debt. In November 1865, Grant visited the South for ten days at the president's request, and reported favorably on the progress of the Johnson program. A month later, when Congress reconvened, the lenient policies of President Johnson immediately came under attack.

In the summer of 1866, Johnson toured the northern states ("Swing around the Circle"), ostensibly to dedicate a monument in Chicago to the late Senator Stephen Douglas of Illinois, but in fact to recruit support for Johnson's reconstruction program. Grant, Rawlins, Admiral Farragut and several other luminaries accompanied him; and Cadwallader was among the newsmen. Rawlins was initially opposed to the trip,[468] but later saw in it an opportunity to expose Grant to the political scene. Besides, the trip would take the two away from the hectic duties in the War Department.

Along the way, the Cleveland Reception Committee provided the presidential party with a refreshment car, loaded with drinks. Grant somehow managed to make his way into the car. After Rawlins and Cadwallader found him, they took him to the baggage car and laid him down on a pile of sacks. The two stood guard against intruders until the train reached Cleveland, and the attention of the presidential party could be diverted.[469]

President Johnson made many speeches and shook many hands, but it soon became apparent that he had failed to enlist public support for his programs. As the tour wore on, the audiences became increasingly hostile. In fact, Grant and Farragut often received more applause than did the president. Grant and Rawlins fled the train in Detroit but rejoined the presidential party in Chicago and went on with Johnson to St. Louis. There, they left the train in disgust.[470]

The trip cured Rawlins of his sympathy for the president, a fellow Democrat, and convinced him that Andrew Johnson would not be a viable candidate in 1868.[471] After all, Rawlins had been a politician of sorts and still retained a keen sense of political reality.

Many problems awaited the two on their return to Washington. The first concerned Robert E. Lee, who was about to be indicted for treason by a Norfolk Grand Jury. Grant maintained that the terms of surrender at Appomattox precluded charges of treason. Rawlins spread the word among the Lee supporters that if Lee were to be convicted, Grant would immediately recommend that the president grant a pardon.[472] The indictment was delivered, but General Lee was never prosecuted.

Rawlins had a long established rule that no letter or report could leave the office of the General of the Army until it had first been examined and approved by him. Grant had written a letter to Sherman which might have had political ramifications. When shown the letter, Rawlins objected to the language and returned it to Grant for revision. Grant complied with the request, but sometime later saw his letter resting in a pigeon hole. He protested to Rawlins that he was competent to manage his own private correspondence and should be allowed to do so. Rawlins gently dissuaded him, and the letter was never sent.[473]

Rawlins and others were deeply concerned with the welfare of the Union soldiers now returned to civilian life. A number of military societies were being formed, among them an association of officers who had served in the Army of the Tennessee. They called themselves the "Society of the Army of the Tennessee" and elected as its first president "General

John A. Rawlins, USA, Chief of Staff to the Lieutenant General, in consideration of his eminent service to our country...and also for his ability for the position."

The first convention was held November 14, 1865 in Cincinnati, Ohio. With Grant and Sherman in attendance, Rawlins delivered an outline of the history of the Army of the Tennessee. He remained the president of the society until his death.

Meanwhile in Danbury his family waited anxiously while Rawlins searched for a suitable home in Washington.

In December 1866, an act was passed over the president's veto establishing a military government in the southern states, to replace the state governments that Johnson had encouraged and that the Congress had repudiated. The bill divided the South into five military departments, each with a commanding officer. While the bill was being debated, Grant let it be known that he preferred that the power of appointment of the district commanders be vested in the president, rather than in the General in Chief. As time passed, Republican office holders were elected or appointed in all the southern states; new state constitutions were written; new state governments formed; and the Fourteenth Amendment was eventually ratified by the southern state legislatures.

Grant had the authority over the military commanders, and Rawlins supervised the administration. When General Winfield Scott Hancock, commander of the Fifth Military District in Louisiana-Texas, arbitrarily removed three black aldermen from office and replaced them with white men, Rawlins ordered the black officials restored *ad interim,* pending the outcome of an election.[474]

Since it was quite apparent that Johnson would not be elected to a second term, a drive was launched by Republican leaders to nominate Grant for the presidency. Although Rawlins had reservations about Grant's suitability, he supported the movement, but to a friend he expressed his opinion that Grant was "not a man of ability outside the profession of arms."[475] Important political leaders came to regard Rawlins as Grant's spokesman. Sherman tried to persuade Grant to remain in the military; Wilson did his best to steer him into politics. Others on the staff opposed a political career. Babcock wrote to Washburne:

> I am one of those who hope General Grant will not be President…I look upon it as a great misfortune to him.

He added that Porter agrees with him.[476]

Since Rawlins' health was noticeably declining, Grant and others were persuaded that his Chief of

Staff might benefit from a change in climate. Arrangements were made for Rawlins and William M. Dunn, his ADC, to accompany General G. M. Dodge, now the chief engineer of the Union Pacific Railroad, on a tour of inspection in the West.

Before leaving, Rawlins composed an address to be delivered at Galena. Grant examined and approved the speech, so it was widely regarded as an exposition of Grant's views. Accordingly, the text was printed and distributed by the Republican Congressional Committee.

While en route to Galena, Rawlins received word from Emma that Willie, their infant son,[477] had died. Rawlins' health was so precarious that he could not turn back. The following day he delivered his speech in Galena, which the *Chicago Tribune* hailed as the "platform of the Republican party."[478]

The speech was critical of Johnson and clearly sided with the radical Republicans. Rawlins recommended that the newly emancipated be given citizenship and suffrage; that civil office be denied to those who had engaged in the insurrection; that civilian government quickly replace military government; that the United States forever repudiate the Confederate debt; that Irish freedom be encouraged; and that British possessions in North America (Canada) be seized, if the British refuse to settle the outstanding Alabama claims. He looked forward "to the departure of the last foreign power from the continent," presumably referring to Spain (Cuba) and Great Britain (Canada).

Rawlins had early espoused the cause of Cuban freedom and would continue to support this movement for the remainder of his life. As time passed, he became a respected figure among the exiled Cuban community, about whom Jose Marti wrote:

…he was dominated by only one passion—justice.[479]

Although the Galena speech was in part compatible with the Radical Republican policy, the disenfranchisement of the former Confederate soldiers differed from Grant's previously expressed sentiments.

Rawlins rested a few days in Galena, where he visited his parents and renewed old friendships. A group of citizens, knowing of Rawlins' dismal financial situation, presented him with a check for one thousand dollars. After Galena, he traveled to Chicago, where he was met by J. Russell Jones and others, all highly supportive of the Galena speech. Jones was the chosen financial advisor of both Grant and Rawlins, so Rawlins entrusted to him the thousand dollars, for investment in street railway shares.

Even as his health was failing, Rawlins kept alive his hopes for recovery. From Chicago, he set out for the West. Accompanying Rawlins, Dunn (ADC) and General Grenville Dodge[480] was Jacob Blikenderfer, who had been sent by President Johnson to determine where the eastern boundary of the Rocky Mountains began. Federal subsidies increased from $16,000 to $48,000 per mile, once the Union Pacific Railroad reached the mountainous area.[481]

The trip took the party to Omaha and then to a new end-of-line town in the Wyoming Territory named Cheyenne. Further west, a cavalry detachment accompanied the train along the newly laid track. Rawlins enjoyed the camps and the camp fare, especially the antelope steak and canned fruit. He participated in bear and bison hunts and had a narrow escape from a grizzly bear and later from a threatened Indian attack. As was his nature, he worried about the health of his companion, General Dodge, who had been wounded in the war and was now sorely overburdened with work. In his official capacity, Rawlins inspected prospective army sites, travelling by horseback over the rough terrain. At one stop in the Wyoming Territory, the party came to a flowing spring from which Rawlins drank with great relish, a veritable oasis in the desert. A town later sprang up on the site, and General Dodge proposed the name "Rawlins," which continues to this day.[482]

They continued over the Continental Divide into Utah. Although the cough continued, Rawlins convinced himself that his health was improving. Brigham Young, the president of the Church of the Latter Day Saints, met the party in Salt Lake City, but they declined his offer of hospitality. While in Salt Lake City, Rawlins learned that President Johnson had appointed Grant as secretary of war and immediately saw the peril. "Had I been there," he lamented, "I might have prevailed upon the General not to accept the position."[483] His forebodings were soon borne out, for the appointment proved a snare for Grant.

After a four month trip in the West, Rawlins returned to Washington in mid-October 1867 and was promptly immersed in the political morass. Congress had enacted a Tenure of Office Act in March 1867, forbidding the president to dismiss any Federal office holder who had been approved by the Senate, without the consent of that body. Notwithstanding, Johnson removed Secretary of War Stanton and in his place appointed Grant, whom Johnson regarded as sympathetic to his views. Grant was compliant at first and defended Johnson's authority, but when Congress reconvened and passed a resolution disapproving Johnson's action, Grant immediately resigned his office and reverted to his army rank.

Johnson denounced Grant's action, maintaining that Grant had promised to remain in office, despite Congressional wish, long enough for the Supreme Court to adjudicate the matter. Rawlins persuaded Grant to publically deny Johnson's assertion, thereby protecting Grant's *bona fides* with the Republican Party. Grant did this in a letter to the president, which Rawlins helped draft. In it, he affirmed that Johnson was attempting "to involve me in a resistance of law for which you [President Johnson] hesitated to assume the responsibility."[484]

Gideon Wells, the secretary of the navy, was somewhat cynical about the affair and wrote in his diary:

> General Grant has become severely afflicted with the Presidential disease, and it warps his judgment, which is not very intelligent or enlightened at best.[485]

In the fall of 1867, a secret Republicans caucus convened to discuss a choice for the presidency. Rawlins and Babcock were present. The conclave unanimously supported the nomination of Grant, with the exception of Charles Sumner, Senator from Massachusetts, himself a presidential hopeful.[486]

Rawlins is said to have been a principal in the National Convention of Soldiers and Sailors, which met May 19th and endorsed Grant for the presidency. Two days later, Grant was unanimously nominated for the presidency by the National Republican Convention on a platform broadly similar to the policies espoused in the Galena speech.

The nomination compelled Grant to resign his position as General of the Army, for which he had been receiving $17,000–20,000 a year.

Grant settled into his new home in Galena during the election, while Rawlins remained in Washington to conduct business.[487] Grant was elected with a majority of 300,000 votes, largely attributable to the 500,000 newly enfranchised black voters in the South. At the age of forty-two, Grant was the youngest president to hold office. Some believed that he accepted his election more as a reward for services than as a responsibility. Observed one historian:

> He had no idea of what it meant to be President of the United States; he did not ever, it soon appeared, understand constitutional law.[488]

After the election, politicians besieged Rawlins with queries on policy and requests for appointments. He bought a house on Montgomery Street in Georgetown Heights. While the alterations were being completed, he declined an invitation to stay with the Grants and slept in his office at the War Department. Later, he shared his house with

Cadwallader, while repairs were in progress. Mornings, he took rides on "Jeff Davis," Grant's black pony, with no discernible benefit to his health.

On Inauguration Day, March 4, 1868 President Johnson refused to accompany Grant to the ceremony, so Rawlins rode beside him in Julia's new phaeton. Grant had been somewhat furtive about his cabinet appointments, and his selections struck many as curious. The turnover was brisk. In all, he appointed twenty-seven men at various times to the seven cabinet offices. Twelve of his relatives were appointed to minor offices.

Rawlins delivered the list of cabinet appointments to the Senate. Washburne was made secretary of state for a brief term of office, before being named as minister to France (his wife was of French descent), a post which he filled with distinction for eight years. The ever intrusive J. Russell Jones was made minister to Belgium; Adam Badeau, a deputy chief of mission (consul) in Britain. Porter and Babcock became White House secretaries. Colonel Jacob D. Cox,[489] recent Governor of Ohio, was named secretary of the interior. Cox had endorsed President Johnson's Reconstruction policy.[490]

Some of the appointments were outstanding. Hamilton Fish, who succeeded Washburne, became a noteworthy secretary of state. George Boutwell, secretary of the treasury, revitalized tax collections and reduced the national debt by redeeming government bonds.[491] Ely Parker was appointed Commissioner of Indian affairs.

Many assumed that Rawlins would be given a cabinet post. When told by Wilson that Grant proposed to offer him command of the Military Department of the Southwest (Arizona Territory), to help restore his health, Rawlins let it be known that he wanted the position of secretary of war. Grant immediately assented, but informed him that he would have to wait a few weeks. News of his appointment reached him in Danbury. Many believed that Grant was anxious to shed the all too prevalent impression that Rawlins was the "indispensable man."[492]

Before the Rawlins appointment was announced, General Dodge and a few friends bought up and returned to Rawlins the mortgage on his Georgetown Heights home.[493] Many Washingtonians were pleased with his appointment. Wells wrote in his diary:

> I have always considered Rawlins as possessing the superior, though not great, mind. His health is not good, but I think his influence will be in the right direction, beneficial for Grant and the administration.[494]

Rawlins began his term of office by settling a disturbing controversy between Sherman and the War Department. His first action as secretary of war was to revoke the order of his predecessor, relinquishing much of the functions of the War Department to General William T. Sherman, now the General-in-Chief. Rawlins firmly maintained that the War Department must remain in civilian hands:

> I could not consent to have the authority of a great civil office entrusted to me subordinated to the military authority.[495]

He convinced Grant that the previous arrangement, by which the civil power of the secretary of war had been entrusted to a military man, would not only discredit the office, but would stir the wrath of Congress. Rawlins prevailed. The Department remained under civilian control, and Sherman remained his friend. Ironically, Sherman would later become the *ad interim* secretary of war, when Rawlins could no longer fulfill his duties.

As time wore on, Grant would have been less than human had he not begun to feel that he was cloaked in some personal greatness or some superior quality, of which even he had been hitherto ignorant.[496] Grant sorely needed advice, but he often treated his cabinet more as clerks than as counselors. Rawlins alone knew the capacities and limitations of the president and never failed to forcefully express his opinion on important matters; and even on subjects not clearly in the purview of the secretary of war. Wilson noted:

> While he held him in the highest respect, stood not in the slightest awe of him or his opinions.[497]

Someone recorded the conversation on one occasion when Rawlins was especially vehement on a particular subject:

Rawlins:

> I have been your adjutant and I think you will excuse me for being earnest!

Grant:

> You are still my adjutant![498]

On several occasions, Rawlins literally left a sick bed to attend a cabinet meeting. Grant was less reserved and more outspoken with him than with the other members of the cabinet.[499] A fellow cabinet officer said of Rawlins:

> He could give warnings that no one else could utter; he could insist upon debate and information before settled purposes should be adopted; he would know of influences at work that others would learn of only when some important step was already taken; his own openness of character would make him frank in action with his colleagues and an honorable representative of their general judgment and policy.[500]

Although not the concern of the secretary of war, Rawlins was "sensitive to injustices done to people who had not the power to defend themselves."[501] He sympathized with the efforts of the Irish to shed British rule and supported just reparations for the *Alabama* claims against Great Britain, arising from the damage inflicted upon Union shipping by the Confederate raider during the Civil War. Frequently, his views clashed with those of Hamilton Fish, the able secretary of state. During his six months of office as secretary of war, his duties were numerous and he signed no fewer than 464 letters.[502]

A strong Cuban exile group had long sought United States intervention in Cuba. Many Americans supported the Cuban cause, among them Charles Dana of the (New York) *Sun*, James Gordon Bennett of the *New York Herald* and Representative John Logan of Illinois. The Cuban exile group issued bonds, which were redeemable once Cuban freedom had been achieved, but subject to approval by the future Cuban government. The bonds were, of course, worthless at the time of issue and had negligible prospects of redemption. In fairness to the historical record, it should be mentioned that Rawlins bought or received $28,000 of Cuban bonds. Smith terms this episode as the first known instance of fiscal irregularity in the Grant administration, and he describes Rawlins as the "first member of Grant's administration to succumb to temptation."[503] This seems excessively harsh, in view of the worthless value of the bonds. More likely, the bonds were forced upon him in circumstances where they could not be refused without giving offense. Closer to the mark are the observations of the great Cuban patriot, Jose Marti, who spent fifteen years in the United States and wrote of Rawlins:

> He could think and act without fear, for he was dominated by only one passion—justice.[504] ...While he was in the cabinet, the thieves and wicked counselors did not cross the threshold.[505]

Because of his declining health, Rawlins left Washington in May and spent six weeks with his family in Danbury. While at home, Rawlins had a pulmonary hemorrhage, but left immediately for Washington when he learned of a forthcoming cabinet session. He had another hemorrhage in New York and again on arrival in Washington, but took his place next to Grant at the cabinet meeting.[506]

At his last cabinet session, he urged that recognition be extended to the provisional government of Cuba.[507] Instead, Grant heeded the advice of Secretary Hamilton Fish and abstained from intervention.

By September, Rawlins was no longer able to visit his office. Important matters were brought to his home.

One of the matters brought to him was the height of the Brooklyn Bridge. As secretary of war, he had the responsibility of insuring that the height of the bridge could accommodate the passage of warships below. The Roeblings proposed a 130 foot height; the ship masters, 140 feet. Rawlins established the height at 135 feet above the high water mark. Ironically, General Sherman helped share the burdens of the office to oblige his friend, becoming, in effect, temporary secretary of war. Of Rawlins, Sherman wrote:

> Rawlins was violent, passionate, enthusiastic and personal, but always in the right direction.[508]

In his final days, Rawlins was moved to the home of General Giles A. Smith,[509] an old comrade, who could better provide care. There, he was attended by Drs. John Hancock Douglas and D. W. Bliss.[510] Emma herself was too ill to travel to Washington. As he lay dying, he dictated his will to Parker, whose loyalty to Rawlins was even greater than to Grant.[511] Rawlins named Grant and Emma as the guardians of the children and executors of his will. He left to his wife and three children his house and lot in Georgetown Heights and a few lots in Wyoming

Territory. The Rawlins homestead in Guilford was left to his father and mother, both of whom survived him. Sherman and Jacob Cox bore witness to the will. James H. Wilson, who had travelled a thousand miles to be present at his last hour, was named as his literary executor. Rawlins expressed a wish to be baptized, and a minister was sent for. His last words expressed a concern for the Union men living in the South and for the struggle for Cuban independence. "Cuba must be free!" he whispered.[512]

Rawlins kept asking for Grant. "Has the old man come yet?" he kept repeating.

"In ten minutes," Sherman assured him.

Grant was in Saratoga with Julia, when at 4:45 p.m. on September 5, 1869 he was handed a telegram from Sherman that Rawlins would not last the day. Grant immediately set out for Washington by train. On his arrival, Sherman and Cox met him on the train platform. By the time they reached the Smith home, Rawlins had been dead for an hour.[513] Grant notified Emma by telegram.[514] The official cause of death was hemorrhage of the lungs, due to pulmonary tuberculosis.

On the day of the funeral service, all Washington was draped in mourning. The bells tolled for two hours, and public offices and businesses were closed.

Wrote a Washington journalist in his dispatch to the *Galena Evening Gazette*:

> Nothing but the death of the lamented Lincoln ever threw so dark a pall of sadness over our entire community.[515]

Funeral services were held in the War Department building. The president attended with the cabinet and diplomatic corps. Army officers wore the badges of mourning. The procession passed the White House and proceeded along E Street to the Congressional Cemetery.

There was no mention of the Cuban bonds in the Rawlins will. They were later found by Grant, who had been named the executor of the Rawlins estate.[516] Grant chose not to disclose the matter, nor could he put the bonds up for sale, since they were worthless and the publicity would discredit the otherwise sterling reputation of his former secretary of war. Some might say that Grant's indifference to Rawlins in the Grant Memoirs springs from this episode; but it is unlikely to be the cause, although in Grant's mind it might have been the justification.

Jacob Dolson Cox, the secretary of the interior, regarded the death of Rawlins as "an irreparable loss" to Grant:

> ...no other man could be found who could be the successful intermediary between General Grant and

his associates in public duty...Rawlins could argue, could expostulate, could condemn and even upbraid without interrupting for an hour the fraternal confidence and good will of Grant.[517]

Allan Nevins, biographer of Hamilton Fish, wrote critically with the wisdom of hindsight:

...he [Rawlins] is the most dangerous member of the original cabinet and his death so frequently described as a disaster, was rather a blessing...While he stayed at Grant's right hand, the peril of war with England and Spain would remain great.[518]

The body was temporarily housed in the public vault of the Congressional Crypt in the Congressional Cemetery. There it remained for two decades, unburied and virtually ignored. Representative John Logan, his old comrade in arms, upbraided the House of Representatives for its neglect.[519] On February 8, 1899, the body was removed to the National Military Cemetery at Arlington, where it now reposes, close by the graves of General Philip Sheridan and Admiral David Porter.

In 1872, Congress appropriated $10,000 for a full length bronze statue of Rawlins, and $3,000 for a pedestal. The sculptor was Joseph A. Bailly, a Pennsylvania artist, born in France. The statue was made of bronze, cast from captured Confederate cannon, and stood eight feet high on a twelve foot pedestal. There was no formal dedication. Over the years, the statue was moved several times before it came to rest in Rawlins Park on 18th and E Streets. A public subscription of fifty thousand dollars was begun by Horace Greeley for Emma and the children of his first wife. It is not likely that the goal was attained. The Cuban exile committee contributed $20,000 of worthless bonds.[520]

Emma applied for a widow's pension and benefits for the minor children.[521] The application was encumbered by the absence of any record of medical disability in the Rawlins file at the Adjutant General's office. Apparently, Rawlins "was never under regular medical treatment by any of the medical officers on duty at this office." In the widow's brief, she submitted a certificate by Dr. Edward. D. Kittoe, who had accompanied Rawlins to Chattanooga.[522] He affirmed that around November 1, 1863, Rawlins "was wetted through with a heavy rain…and not being properly cared for owing to the condition of affairs at Chattanooga, he contracted a severe attack of bronchitis from which he only partially recovered. When about the 25th or 30th of November, while at Chattanooga, he slept in a damp tent which aggravated his case and from this time symptoms of pulmonary consumption appeared and continued to be more and more fully developed until eventually death ensued in consequence"[523]

Emma was granted a monthly pension of $20.[524] Orville Babcock, Grant's secretary, notified her that he had paid the assessment on the Georgetown Heights home and had obtained for it a home insurance policy for $5,000. Grant sent her a check for $1,155 for monies accrued to the estate. On August 17, 1870 Grant wrote to Emma that the trust would pay an additional $11,000 for a new home in Danbury on 17 Balmford Avenue, which the newspapers described as having a Second Empire style and a mansard roof.[525] In 1872, Emma married Charles F. Daniels and divorced him on March 2, 1874. She wrote to the commander of a Grand Army of the Republic post in Washington in 1873 to request that he decorate the tomb of John Rawlins at the Congressional Cemetery.[526] Emma survived John A. Rawlins by four years. She died from tuberculosis on November 6, 1874 in Cheyenne, Wyoming Territory, where she owned lots deeded by her first husband. Her body was taken to Danbury for burial in the Hurlburt family plot.

All three children born to Emma Hurlburt Rawlins (Willie, Mary and Violet) died in infancy. The three children born to Emily Smith Rawlins were raised by Miss Sarah Smith, her sister. Following Emma's death, Hiram Smith, uncle of the surviving children, applied for guardianship in December 1874, so that he could apply on their behalf for an army pension.

The oldest surviving child, James Bradner Rawlins, was appointed by President Grant to the Military Academy at West Point. He was the only presidential appointment to pass the entrance exam. Although an outstanding cadet in his freshman year, sadly he developed seizures, possibly a residuum of tubercular meningitis, which compelled his withdrawal from the Academy. The seizures continued, followed later by blindness, which precluded gainful employment. A small dependant's pension of $30 per month was awarded him by the House of Representatives in a directive to the secretary of the interior. He lived with his sister Jennie Holman, in Toms River, New Jersey, and died in a sanatorium on January 21, 1917. He was buried in nearby Phillipsburg, New York, beside his mother. His sister, Emily, remained in the Smith home, as a ward of General Grant and later married Dr. Wesley Wait of Newburg. The other daughter, Jennie, married George W. Holman, Jr. of New York City on September 6, 1882. Grant was unable to attend either wedding.[527]

Of the nine Rawlins siblings, the children of James and Lovisa Rawlins, all five surviving children[528] achieved an honorable station in life.[529]

Rawlins' successor in office was William W. Belknap, who fought at Shiloh and Vicksburg and commanded a division in Sherman's Army. He would bring shame to the Grant administration from his wife's involvement in the sale of Indian agencies. Also connected to that scandal were Orville Grant and John D. Dent, (Julia's brother).[530]

Grant was reelected to a second term. His administrations were plagued by the *Credit Mobilier*-Union Pacific Railroad scandal (which began during the Johnson administration); the Belknap Indian agent bribery scandal; the Whiskey Ring tax evasion scandal involving Orville Babcock,[531] Grant's private secretary; the gold scandal; the back pay grab; and the abortive San Domingo annexation.

Throughout his two terms of office, President Grant strove to aid and protect the black population. The Civil Rights Act of 1875 is said to be the strongest civil rights legislation enacted in the interval between the administrations of Abraham Lincoln and Lyndon Johnson. Among the other redeeming features of Grant's administration: civil rights were restored to nearly every ex-Confederate; the *Alabama* claims were settled by an arbitration tribunal, which became an important template for the settlement for international disputes; the San Juan boundary claim was settled with Canada; the transcontinental railroad was completed; and a well-intentioned Indian peace policy was established through the offices of Ely Parker, Commissioner of Indian Affairs. Unfortunately, the initiatives herded the Indian tribes implacably toward the reservation, governmental dependence and agriculture. The Indians became wards of the United States but were not given citizenship until 1931.

Ely Parker brought a breath of fresh air to the Indian Affairs Department. Indents were expedited and disreputable Indian treaties reexamined. In contrast to his predecessors who awarded contracts for gain, Parker insisted on public bidding. Heretofore, only twenty percent of the appropriated monies ever reached the intended recipients. Despite his best efforts, the bidding was often rigged, and the supplies deficient both in quality and quantity.

Parker lasted two years as Commissioner of Indian Affairs and then resigned after politically motivated charges were brought against him, alleging that he had purchased emergency food and supplies for the Plains Indians without approval by the president or by other members of the Commission.[532] Congress investigated and determined that he had not personally profited in the least from his actions.

A brief word about some of the others intimates of Rawlins:

Charles Dana became editor of the *Chicago Republican* and later the *New York Sun*. He supported Grant for the presidency in 1868 but later opposed him, when Grant failed to appoint him Commissioner of the New York Customs.

Sylvanus Cadwallader became a New York bureau chief of the *New York Herald* and later assistant secretary of state for Wisconsin. His memoirs were written in 1896 but went unpublished until 1955.[533]

James H. Wilson resigned from the army in 1870. He entered the business world and travelled extensively. Reentering the military during the Spanish American War, he served in Puerto Rico and then during the Boxer Rebellion.

Ulysses S. Grant died of throat cancer on July 23, 1885. His tomb, the largest in North America, was built at a cost of $800,000 and was patterned after the Napoleon Mausoleum at *Les Invalides* in Paris. Sadly, in the century which followed, Grant's Tomb was allowed to become "an undervisited, underfunded and ignored national monument."[534] The graffiti has since been erased and the grass cut; but attendance remains sparse. Encircling the sarcophagi of Ulysses and Julia Grant are busts of Generals Sherman, Thomas, Sheridan, McPherson and Ord. Nowhere in this rather sterile mausoleum is there mention of the man who walked beside Grant down the narrow path to glory.

Statue of Rawlins in Rawlins Park, Washington, D.C.
Library of Congress

NOTES

CHM Chicago Historical Museum

LC Library of Congress

NA National Archives

INTRODUCTION

[1] See section on Alcohol in *Ulysses S. Grant: A Bibliography*, N.Y.: Praeger, 2005; Marie Kelsey. http://faculty.css.edu/mkelsey/usgrant/alcohol.htm.
[2] Wilson, 61.
[3] Grant, Julia, *Memoirs,* 22.
[4] Brinton, 137.

EARLY YEARS

[5] Named for Joseph Hamilton Daviess of Kentucky, killed 1811 at Tippecanoe.

[6] First regular store built 1829 by Frederic Dent of St. Louis, father-in-law of U. S. Grant. (*Harper's Monthly*, May 1866).

[7] *Chicago Tribune*, April 17, 1892.

[8] *Galena Weekly*, July 1893.

[9] *Galena Weekly*, July 1893

[10] "He [John Rawlins] would rather see a friend of his take a glass of poison than a glass of whiskey." Wilson, 25.

[11] Died July 21, 1893; wife died July 18, 1891.

[12] *Harper's New Monthly Magazine*, May 1866, 681.

[13] Chetlain, 46.

[14] Walker, Keith, *Charcoal in the Forest of Dean*, http://www.fweb.org.uk/Dedan/deanhist/charcoal.htm; also Charcoal Wikipedia.org.

[15] 1834-1895

[16] Rawlins boarded at the home of the Rev. H. Crews (Galena City Directory 1854).

[17] Chetlain, 278.

[18] Born February 25, 1804; died October 10, 1866.

[19] Born May 18, 1808; died November 26, 1885.

[20] *Chicago Tribune*, April 17, 1892.

[21] Chetlain, 93.

[22] The 1860 Census lists the ages of James, three years; Jennie, one year and Emily, two months.

[23] Census of 1860.

[24] Lewis, 381.

[25] Their office was located at Hill and Main Streets (Galena City Directory 1858-59).

[26] Richardson, 169.

[27] Washburne, Vol. 1, 358.

[28] Church, Charles, *History of Rockford and Winnebago County, Illinois*, New England Society of Rockford. Illinois, Rockford: Lamb, 1900, 378.

29 Jones arrived in Galena in 1838 with a dollar in his pocket. In short order he rose to be manager of a dry goods store, then partner of the store and manager of a steamship company. (Lewis, 406).
30 *NY Times*, October 24, 1887.
31 Chetlain, 38.
32 Cadwallader, 208.
33 Wilson, 48.
34 It was said that Winston Churchill was considered so hopelessly incompetent in the classics that English literature was substituted in his curriculum.
35 Emma Dent Casey in *Ulysses S. Grant Association Newsletter*, July 1968.
36 Lewis, 262.
37 Charles S. Tripler, *Ulysses S. Grant Association Newsletter*, October 1967.
38 Ibid., 316.
39 Ibid., 328.
40 Grant returned by way of Nicaragua, travelling twelve miles by carriage, fifty miles by boat on Lake Nicaragua and 125 miles up the San Juan River to Punta Arenas on the Atlantic Ocean.
41 Lewis, 5.
42 "How Grant Got to Know Rawlins," *Army and Navy Journal*, September 12, 1868, 53; Fred Grant, *Ulysses S. Grant Association Newsletter*, January 1972.
43 Chetlain, 65.
44 Richardson, 161.
45 Ibid, 295.
46 Statement of Melancthron Burke, Hamlin Garland Papers, Doheny Library, University of Southern California.
47 James Sanderson, *U.S. Grant Newsletter*, January 1964.
48 Died in 1861.

49 *Wisconsin Magazine of History*, State Historical Society of Wisconsin, Vol. 3, 85.
50 Harland, Hamlin, "Grant on the Outbreak of the War" in *McClure Magazine*, Vol. 9, 1897, p. 603.
51 Richardson, 165.
52 Grant, Julia, 82.
53 Fred Grant, *Ulysses S. Grant Association Newsletter*, January 1972; Julia Grant, 84.
54 Statement of Melancthron Burke, Hamlin Garland Papers, Donheny Library, University of Southern California.
55 Parker, Ely. "The Character of Grant," in *Personal Recollections of the War*, J. G. Wilson and T. M. Coan, Series I, N.Y., 1891, 355.
56 Ibid., 389.
57 Armstrong, 74; also, Parker, 96. The incident is said to have been described in a letter that no longer exists.
58 Lewis, 408.
59 Woodward, 206.
60 Shaw, 383-5.
61 Chetlain, 75.
62 Lewis, 319.
63 Emerson, John, "Grant's Life in the West" in *Midland Monthly*, January 1898, 51.
64 McPherson, *Battle Cry,* 588.
65 His wife, Hannah, was a firm Democrat.
66 Richardson, 180.
67 Rawlins Interview, *Army and Navy Journal*, September 12, 1868.
68 Grant to Julia, August 10, 1861 in Ulysses S. Grant, *Memoirs and Selected Letters*, 974.
69 The Adjutant General, Lorenzo Thomas, was stationed in Washington.
70 Grant to Washburne, September 3, 1861 in Wilson, 55.

WAR IN THE WEST

[71] Later, the District of Cairo.
[72] Crozier, 191.
[73] Joseph Wham, *Ulysses S. Grant Association Newsletter*, January 1968.
[74] Marazalek, 157.
[75] Brinton, 30.
[76] Rawlins Interview, *Army and Navy Journal*, September 12, 1868.
[77] Ibid., 326.
[78] *Midland Monthly*, March 1898, 226.
[79] *Army and Navy Journal*, September 12, 1868.
[80] Brinton, 38.
[81] Sherman, Hoyt, in *Midland Monthly*, April, 1898, 326
[82] Richardson, Albert D., *A Personal History of Ulysses S. Grant*, Hartford, 1868, 189.
[83] Longacre, 95.
[84] Brinton, 130.
[85] Cadwallader, 118.
[86] Cadwallader, in Wilson, *Rawlins*, 429.
[87] Locke, Frederick T., "Recollections of an Adjutant-General" in Wilson and Coan, *Personal Recollections*, I: 42 Armstrong, 88.
[88] Anderson, 205.
[89] OR, Series I, Vol. III, Chap. X, 267; Grant, *Personal Memoirs (two vol. in one), Vol. 1*, 160.
[90] U. S. Grant *Memoirs and Selected Letters*, N.Y.: Library of America, 1990, 178.
[91] McFeeley, 92.
[92] Conger, 66.
[93] OR, Series `1, Vol. 3, Chap. X, 271-351.
[94] Hughes and Cheairs, 121.
[95] Hughes and Cheairs, 266 n.33.

[96] Richardson, 194.
[97] Conger, 94.
[98] Miers, 14.
[99] Korda, 68.
[100] Anderson and Anderson, 212.
[101] Hurst, 93.
[102] Grant, Julia, 93.
[103] Simpson, 110.
[104] Grant, Julia, 94.
[105] Cadwallader, 119.
[106] Buell, 151.
[107] Cadwallader statement, in Wilson, *Rawlins,* 430.
[108] Grant, Julia, 46.
[109] Buell, 150.
[110] Simpson, 176.
[111] Greenbie, 178.
[112] Rawlins to Washburne, December 30, 1861, Washburne Papers, LC.
[113] Brinton, 138.
[114] J. Russell Jones to E. B. Washburne, January 17, 1862 in Washburne Papers, LC.
[115] Lincoln, himself, wanted activity on the Tennessee River, to relieve pressure on Buell. (Conger, 137).
[116] Bonekemper III, 26.
[117] Ibid., 430.
[118] Crozier, 195.
[119] Grant, Julia, 96.
[120] Brinton, 136; Richardson, 354.
[121] Some time later Grant visited the 21st Illinois Infantry, his old regiment. The men proceeded to cut off locks from the tail and mane, as souvenirs of his visit. Grant departed quickly. Richardson, 204.

[122] Conger, 161.
[123] Rawlins. Address to the Society of the Army of Tennessee, Nov. 14, 1865 in Wilson, 439.
[124] *Midland Monthly*, June 1899, p. 515.
[125] Eisenschiml and Newman, 161.
[126] It was Grant who stated in his memoirs that he saw rations for three days in one of the captured knapsacks (Grant, *Memoirs two vol. in one*), Vol. 1, 181). Apparently, the enemy had not issued travelling rations at that time, so his account is somewhat apocryphal. (Conger, 304).
[127] *Harpers Weekly*, March 8, 1862.
[128] Conger, 155.
[129] Wilson, 72.
[130] Webster, a graduate of Dartmouth, had been a regular army engineer before the war.
[131] Conger, 233.
[132] Buell had sent a division (Nelson) to aid Grant at Donelson, but it arrived too late, and Grant sent it back. The division arrived at Nashville and entered the town, occupying it for the Union. Who should be credited with the occupation of Nashville—Grant or Buell? Buell at the time was still on the other side of the Cumberland River.
[133] *N.Y. Times*, March 5, 1862.
[134] Buell, 168.
[135] Halleck to McClellan, March 4, 1862 in Wilson, 74.
[136] *Midland Monthly*, September 1898, 28.
[137] Richardson, 232.
[138] Wilson, 79.
[139] Brinton, 238; Simpson, *Grant*, 458.
[140] On the eve of battle, McClernand was promoted to Major General. In a few days, he would have been senior to Sherman.
[141] Confederates preferred the name Battle of Pittsburg Landing.

142 Conger, 220.
143 Conger, 221.
144 McFeeley, 112.
145 Rawlins, *Address*, in Wilson, 448.
146 Daniel, 245.
147 Ibid., 260.
148 Macartney, 59.
149 Hurst, 388.
150 *Battle and Leaders of the Civil War*, 1, 610.
151 Born in New Hampshire and a graduate of Dartmouth College, Colonel Webster had served in the regular army as an engineer.
152 Buell arrived in the afternoon, but ferrying his troops took time.
153 Grant, Memoirs, I, 85.
154 Marszalek, 148.
155 Griffin, 96. A total of 1,200 officers served in the pre-war army. Nine hundred remained in the U.S. Army.
156 Marszalek, 122.
157 Grant, Julia, 101.
158 Hurst, 366.
159 Grant, Julia, 116 n. 31.
160 Called a "troop" after 1883.
161 Grant, Julia, 104.
162 Richardson, 202.
163 Cadwallader, 20.
164 Ibid., 57.
165 Cadwallader, 116.
166 Catton, *South*, 395, quotes C. S. Hamilton to Senator Doolittle, October 22, 1863.
167 The price of cotton sold in Memphis rose to as much as $1.10 at one time. Jones to Washburne, February 15, 1863. Washburne Papers, LC.

168. *Collected Works of Abraham Lincoln*, January 5, 1865, Lincoln to R. E. Coxe, Vol. VIII, 189.
169. Badeau, 409.
170. Lincoln to William Kellogg, June 8, 1863 in Dana, *Recollections,* 17: "The officers of the army, in numerous instances, are believed to connive and share the profits…"
171. Jones to Cadwallader, February 15, 1863, Washburne Papers, LC.
172. Wilson, 96.
173. Julia Grant described the order as "obnoxious." Julia Grant, 107.
174. Richardson, 276.
175. Grant, Julia, 148.
176. Wilson graduated sixth in the 1860 Class, McPherson graduated first.
177. Jenney 263, "Personal Recollections of Vicksburg" in *Military Essays and Recollections*, Vol. III, 1894.
178. Grant, Julia, 105.
179. Hamlin Garland interview of James H. Wilson, March 1897 mms. University of South California quoted in Longacre, 156.
180. Grant to Halleck, December 14, 1862 in Papers of USG, 7: 28.
181. Shannon, 159, 265.
182. Rawlins to Sheean, no date, in Wilson, 103.
183. Grant, Julia, 105.
184. Colonel Webster was made superintendant of railroads. His engineering duties were assumed by Col. James McPherson; the artillery, by Col. William Duff.
185. Cox, *Reminiscences,* 164.
186. Korda, 84.
187. Richardson, 294.
188. Cadwallader, 49.
189. Jenney, 257.
190. Simpson, *Grant,* 460.
191. Miers, 88.
192. Wilson, *Dana,* 200,

[193] Cadwallader, 53.
[194] Wilson, *Dana*, 202.
[195] Cadwallader, 61
[196] Dana, "General Grant's Occasional Intoxication" (editorial), *NY Sun*, April 28, 1891.
[197] Wilson, 124.
[198] Miers, 138.
[199] Dana, 63.
[200] Armstrong, 94.
[201] Cadwallader to his wife, May 21, 1863: "the plan, although suggested by Rawlins and Wilson…" Cadwallader, 87.
[202] Grant's *Memoirs two vol. in one,* Vol. 1, 272.
[203] Rawlins to Washburne, February 27, 1863, Washburne Papers, LC.
[204] Cadwallader, 119.
[205] Miers, 140.
[206] Badeau, 182.
[207] Sherman, William T., *Memoirs*, 317.
[208] J. Russell Jones to Washburne, February 5, 1863 in Washburne Papers, LC.
[209] Ibid.
[210] Ibid., 318.
[211] Miers, 158.
[212] Richardson, 309.
[213] Wilson, 127.
[214] Porter, Horace, "*Grant. Personal Recollections of the War of the Rebellion*, [editors] James G. Wilson and Tilas M. Coan, Series I, N.Y.: Commandory Military Order of the Loyal Legion, 1891, 368.
[215] Ibid., 369.
[216] Wilson, Edmund, *Patriotic Gore*, 143.
[217] Sherman, 334.
[218] Miers, 44.
[219] Dana, 54.

[220] Obituary of F. D. Grant, http://www.bilbrary.msstate.edu/usgrant/fdg-obit.asp.
[221] Porter *Campaigning,* 363; Frederick D. Grant, *Ulysses S. Grant Association Newsletter,* October 1969.
[222] Groom, 197.
[223] Dana, 74.
[224] Cadwallader, 70.
[225] Ibid., 241
[226] Jenney, "Personal Recollections of Vicksburg," in *Military Essays and Recollections,* Vol. III, 1894, 261.
[227] Green, 68.
[228] Wilson *Dana,* 211.
[229] Griffin, 74.
[230] Badeau, 391.
[231] Perret, suggests a homoerotic relationship between Wilson and Badeau, 293.
[232] *Ulysses S. Grant Association Newsletter,* October 1965.
[233] Miers, 219.
[234] Ibid., 239.
[235] Rawlins to Grant, June 6, 1863 in Wilson, 463.
[236] Macartney, 84.
[237] 1825-1909.
[238] Sylvanus Cadwallader, *"Three Years with Grant,"* N.Y.: Knopf, 1955.
[239] Dana, *Recollections of the Civil War,* N.Y.: Appleton, 1898.
[240] Wilson, Edmund, *Gore,* 144.
[241] Cadwallader, 102-110.
[242] Owned by Lt. Col. Clark Lagow.
[243] Cadwallader wrote the story in 1896, eight years after Grant's death, but it was not until 1955 that the account was published.
[244] In addition to the fact that Dana denied to Wilson that Cadwallader was present.

245 Richardson, 351.
246 Wilson, 145.
247 Cadwallader, 119.
248 William Samuel Lum died in 1856. Mrs. Anna Maria Owings Lum died in 1870. They had seven children.
249 The Lum House was later ordered to be demolished by Sherman "as a military necessity." By Christmas 1863, the house was rubble.
250 Cadwallader, 123.
251 Walker, 19.
252 *Danbury News-Times*, Sunday, July 14, 1894.
253 *Danbury News-Times*, Sunday, July 14, 1894.
254 Rollins, John Rodman, *Record of Families of the name Rawlins or Rollins in the United States*, 295.
255 Grant, Julia, 119.
256 Schutz, Duane, *The Most Glorious Fourth*, p. 391.
257 Julia Dent Grant, *Recollections*, 120; Drake, Rebecca Blanchard in http://batteof raymond.org/history/lum.htm.
258 Cadwallader, 69.
259 Cadwallader, 125.
260 *Letters of U. S. Grant,* 9: 219.
261 Wells, *Diary*, July 31, 1863, Vol. I, 386.
262 Parker, 95.
263 Armstrong, 89.
264 Col. J. D. Webster, former chief of staff, was made superintendant of railroads.
265 Wilson, 327.
266 *U. S. Grant Memoirs and Selected Letters*, 1034.
267 Grant to Washburne, August 30, 1863 in *USG Memoires and Selected Letters,* 1034.
268 April 4, 1864.
269 Wilson, 139.
270 Cadwallader, in Wilson, 431.

[271] Green, 128.
[272] William Rowley to Washburne, November 20, 1863 in *Papers of USG*, VI: 32.
[273] Catton, *South*, 209.
[274] Wilson, 156.
[275] Wilson, 154.
[276] Wilson, 157.
[277] He did not attend West Point.
[278] Rawlins to Emma Hurlburt, October 9, 1863, CHM.
[279] Rawlins to Emma, October 12, 1863 Rawlins Papers, Chicago Historical Society.
[280] Rawlins to Emma, October 18, 1863, Rawlins Papers, CHM.
[281] Rawlins to Emma, November 16, 1863, Rawlins Papers, CHM.
[282] Rawlins to Emma Hurlburt, November 16, 1863, Rawlins Papers, CHM.
[283] Armstrong, 90.
[284] Buell, 279.
[285] McFeely, 145.
[286] Rawlins to Emma, November 10, 1863, Rawlins Papers, CHS.
[287] Rawlins to Emma, November 21, 1863, Rawlins Letters, CHM.
[288] Macartney, 285.
[289] Rawlins to Washburne, November 14, 1863, Washburne Papers, LC.
[290] Catton, *Command*, 66.
[291] Diary of William W. Smith, November 29, 1863, cited in Simpson *Grant* 280; Catton, *Command*, 115.
[292] R. to Emma, November 16, 1863, Rawlins Papers, CHM.
[293] Rawlins to Emma, November 21, 1863, Rawlins Papers, CHM.
[294] Rawlins to Emma, November 23, 1865, Rawlins Papers, CHM.
[295] R. to Emma, November 23, 1863, Rawlins Papers, CHM.
[296] Arthur MacArthur, father of Gen. Douglas MacArthur, planted the Union flag on the summit.
[297] Wilson, J. H., *Flag*, N.Y.: Appleton, 1912, 1: 157.

[298] Cadwallader, 140.
[299] R. to Emma, December 8, 1863, Rawlins Papers, CHM.
[300] R. to Emma, December 3, 1863, Rawlins Papers, CHM.
[301] Hurd, 240.
[302] Temple, 517.
[303] Grant, Julia, 124.
[304] He first obtained permission (Grant, *Memoirs, two vol. in one*, vol. 2, 401).
[305] The boy recovered after being given a dose of *nux vomica* (Julia Grant, 126).
[306] Schofield, 111.
[307] Catton, *South*, 115.
[308] Rawlins to Emma, January 31, 1863 in Rawlins Papers, CHS.
[309] Rawlins to Wilson, March 3, 1863 in Wilson, 187.
[310] Except for Belmont.
[311] Wilson, 179.
[312] Badeau, 569.
[313] Rawlins to Washburne, January 20, 1864 in Huntington Library, Colbet Collection, cited in Catton, *Command*, 118.
[314] Rawlins to Wilson, March 3, 1864 in Wilson, 184.
[315] Grant to Washburne, January 20, 1864 in USG papers, 9: 543; Simpson, 255.
[316] Wilson, 190.
[317] Rawlins to Washburne, January 20, 1864 in Washburne Papers, LC.
[318] Grant to Sherman, March 10, 1864 in Wilson, 189.
[319] Sherman, *Memoires*, I, 399.

WAR IN THE EAST

[320] Rawlins to Wilson, March 6, 1864 in Wilson, 401.
[321] He visited army headquarters, then Georgetown (in search of Halleck), then back to the Willard Hotel. The next day he visited

Halleck's office, then, Stanton's office; then, the White House. (Simpson, 270).

[322] R. to Emma, March 9, 1864, in Wilson, 403.
[323] Marshall-Cornwall, 139.
[324] Porter, *Campaigning*, 31.
[325] Julia Dent, 199 n. 16.
[326] Dana, 74.
[327] Grant, *Memoirs, two vol. in one,* vol. 2, 408.
[328] Buell, 302.
[329] Wilson, 195.
[330] Schofield, 323.
[331] Wilson, 197.
[332] Wilson, 197.
[333] Rawlins to Wilson, March 28, 1864 in Wilson, 177.
[334] Rawlins to Emma, April 13, 1864 in Wilson, 416.
[335] Catton, South, 174.
[336] Grant, *Memoirs, two vol. in one,* Vol. 2, 412.
[337] Grant did this because Burnside had more seniority than the other generals and would have felt slighted to be under Meade's command.
[338] Rhea, 9.
[339] Rhea, 9.
[340] Wilson, 217.
[341] Burne, 16.
[342] Diary, Marsena Patrick, May 6, 1864, cited in Perrot, 312.
[343] Rhea, 331.
[344] Porter, *Campaigning*, 41.
[345] Simpson, 416. Grant also owned "Jeff Davis," which had an easy gait. (Porter, *Campaigning,* 89).
[346] Porter, *Campaigning*, 41.
[347] Ibid., 83.

[348] Wilson was now cavalry division commander, after having served ten weeks of desk work in Washington.
[349] Buell, 314.
[350] Rawlins to Emma, May 9, 1864 in Wilson, *Rawlins*, 218.
[351] Rawlins to Emma, May 11, 1864 in Wilson, *Rawlins*, 218.
[352] Grant to Halleck, May 11, 1864 in Porter, 97.
[353] Cadwallader, 70.
[354] "General Grant knows that he [Duff] is not the right person [for the job], but it is one of his weaknesses that he is unwilling to hurt the feelings of a friend and so he keeps him on." Dana, *Recollections*, 74.
[355] Catton, *Command*, 223.
[356] Rawlins to Emma, May 2, 1864 in Wilson, 427.
[357] Rhea, 9.
[358] Smith did cut a few miles of Petersburg-Richmond track, which was easily repaired.
[359] Rawlins to Emma, May 26, 1864, Wilson, 221.
[360] Rhea, 10.
[361] Rawlins to Emma, May 25, 1864 in Wilson, *Rawlins*, 220.
[362] Rawlins to Emma, May 28, 1864 in Wilson, *Rawlins*, 222.
[363] Rawlins to Emma, May 29, 1864 in Wilson, *Rawlins*, 223.
[364] OR Vol. XXXVI, Part 3, 317.
[365] Rawlins to Emma, May 30, 1864 in Wilson, *Rawlins*, 224.
[366] Smith was mistakenly ordered to proceed to New Castle, instead of Cold Harbor (Marshall-Cornivall, 174).
[367] Ibid., 173.
[368] Lyman, Meade's Headquarters, 90.
[369] Buell, 336.
[370] Foote, III, 284.
[371] Rawlins to Emma, June 4, 1864 in Wilson Papers, LC.
[372] Green, 124.
[373] Rawlins to Emma, June 8, 1864 in Wilson, *Rawlins*, 229.

874 Except for the later crater attack.
875 Furgurson, 252.
876 Furgurson, 252.
877 Rawlins to Emma, June 17, 1864 in Wilson, *Rawlins,* 234.
878 Woodward, W. E., 275.
879 Rawlins to Emma, June 24, 1864 in Wilson, *Rawlins,* 237.
880 Rawlins to Emma, June 26, 1864 in Wilson, *Rawlins,* 238.
881 Shannon, 278.
882 Rawlins to Emma, June 29, 1864 in Wilson, *Rawlins,* 239.
883 Ibid., July 2, 1864, in Wilson, *Rawlins,* 240.
884 Rawlins to Emma, July 22, 1864 in Wilson, *Rawlins,* 248.
885 Dana to Rawlins, July 14, 1864, Grant Papers XI, 252.
886 Griffin, 118.
887 Rawlins to Emma, July 11, 1863 in Wilson, *Rawlins,* 243.
888 Butler denied the drunk story. Butler, 698.
889 Catton, *Command,* 334. Catton finds difficulties with the story.
890 Macartney, 216.
891 Hesseltine, William B., *Ulysses S. Grant Politician,* 44.
892 Rawlins to Emma, July 28, 1864 in Wilson, *Rawlins,* 249.
893 Rawlins to Emma, July 23, 1864 in Wilson, *Rawlins,* 248.
894 Macartney, 61.
895 Rawlins to Emma, July 28, 1864 in Wilson, *Rawlins,* 249.
896 Catton, *Command,* 320.
397 Williams, T. Harry, 329
398 "Letters of Col. Theodore Lyman," August 9, 1864 in *Atlantic Monthly Press,* 1922, p. 210.
399 Parker, 120.
400 Parker, 131.
401 E. Parker to J. E. Smith, October 15, 1864 quoted in Armstrong, 103.
402 Parker, 114; Porter, 208.
403 Catton, *Command,* 370.
404 Bowers to Rawlins, August 25, 1864 in Wilson, *Rawlins,* 258.

[405] Julia Grant, 162.
[406] Trudeau, *The Last Citadel*, 160.
[407] Porter, 314.
[408] Grant to Julia, October 26, 1864 in *USG Memoirs and Selected Letters*, 1070.
[409] Rawlins to Emma, October 3, 1864 in Wilson, *Rawlins*, 264.
[410] Wilson, 249.
[411] Porter, 279.
[412] Butler, 696.
[413] Catton, *Command*, 427.
[414] Rawlins to Emma, October 10, 1864 in Wilson, *Rawlins*, 264.
[415] Cadwallader to Wilson, October 12, 1904 in Wilson Papers, LC.
[416] Porter, *Campaigning*, 318.
[417] R. to Emma, October15, 1864 in Wilson, *Rawlins*, 266.
[418] R. to Emma, October 13, 1864 in Wilson, *Rawlins*, 265.
[419] Porter, *Campaigning*, 314.
[420] Ibid., 314.
[421] Cadwallader, 254.
[422] R. to Emma, November 19, 1864 in Wilson, *Rawlins*, 281.
[423] *Grant Memoirs, two vol. in one*, N.Y.: Webster, 1894, II, 370.
[424] Cadwallader, 255.
[425] Sherman repeats the charge that Rawlins went to Washington to obtain an order, etc. in *Battles and Leaders of the Civil War*, Vol. IV, 157.
[426] Sherman to A. N. Klattenburg, November 13, 1887. Sherman Papers, CMS.
[427] Porter, *Campaigning*, 316.
[428] Cox, *Reminiscences*, vol. 2, 319.
[429] Porter, *Campaigning*, 319.
[430] R. to Emma, October 10, 1864 in Wilson, *Rawlins*, 264.
[431] Ibid., October 13, 1864 in Wilson, *Rawlins*, 265.
[432] R. to Emma, October 16, 1864 in Wilson, *Rawlins*, 266.

[433] Ibid., 267. John Antrobus, born in England, settled in Philadelphia. He was the first artist to paint Grant.
[434] Rosencrans was later replaced by Gen. Grenville Dodge, who sent 15,000 troops to Thomas.
[435] Cadwallader in Wilson, 431.
[436] O.R. Vol 39, part 3, p. 684. cited in Cox, Jacob D., *Military Reminiscences of the Civil War*. http:..www.fullboks.com/Military Reminiscences of the Civil War, Chap. 43.
[437] Wilson, *Rawlins,* 275.
[438] R. to Emma, November 17, 1864 in Wilson, *Rawlins,* 280.
[439] Wilson, *Rawlins,* 282.
[440] Reeder, 187.
[441] Buell, 406.
[442] Ibid., 300.
[443] Cadwallader, 279.
[444] Cadwallader, 202.
[445] Butler to Rawlins, January 13, 1865 in Butler, Appendix, 1130.
[446] Rawlins to Emma, December 1, 1864 in Wilson, *Rawlins,* 288.
[447] R. to Emma, November 25, 1864 in Wilson, *Rawlins,* 285.
[448] Ibid., 303
[449] Griffin, 40.
[450] He had been made Brig. Gen. Volunteers, August 11, 1863.
[451] Porter, *Campaigning,* 411; Sheridan, Vol. 2, 129.
[452] Griffith, Paddy, *Battle Tactics*, New Haven: Yale Univ., 2001, 40.
[453] Porter, *Campaigning,* 427.
[454] Griffin, 181.
[455] Anderson and Anderson, 426.
[456] Grant, *Personal Memoirs*, N.Y.: Dover, 411.
[457] Grant to Sheridan, March 30, 1865 in Sheridan Vol. 2, 142.
[458] Grant, Julia, 148.
[459] Armstrong, 108.
[460] Cadwallader, 318.

[461] Porter, 492.
[462] Flood, 322.
[463] Anderson and Anderson, 6.

FINAL DAYS

[464] Schofield, 379.
[465] Wilson, 327.
[466] Flood, *Grant and Sherman*, 363.
[467] Cadwallader, 119.
[468] McFeely, 251.
[469] Cadwallader, 340.
[470] Ibid., 341.
[471] Wilson to Washburne, October 13, 1866, Washburne Papers, LC.
[472] Simpson, *Grant*, 450.
[473] Wilson, *Rawlins*, 431.
[474] Jordan, 211.
[475] *Browning Diary*, October 25, 1866, Vol. II, 103.
[476] Babcock to Washburne, October 9, 1869 in Washburne Papers, LC.
[477] Emma was his mother.
[478] Wilson, *Rawlins*, 341.
[479] Marti, Jose, 13. Marti, the great champion of Cuban independence, spent fifteen years in the United States as a journalist.
[480] General Dodge had succeeded Rosencrans in St. Louis at the time when Rawlins was recruiting troops for Thomas.
[481] Williams, John H., 170.
[482] Rawlins Springs was the name first proposed.
[483] Rawlins to Emma, August 19, 1866 in Wilson, 344.
[484] Badeau, *Grant in Peace*, 114.
[485] *Diary of Gideon Wells*, August 22, 1867, Vol. III, 180.
[486] Donald, 339.

[487] James D. Rawlins voted for Horace Greeley rather than for Grant, in the 1872 election. (*Galena Weekly*, July 17, 1893).
[488] Wilson, Edmund, *Gore*, 164.
[489] Cox was a graduate of Oberlin College and a distinguished lawyer. He commanded a division in Sherman's Army.
[490] McFeeley, 300.
[491] Smith, 478.
[492] Macartney, 97.
[493] Wilson, *Rawlins*, 353.
[494] *Diary of Gideon Welles*, March 11, 1869, Vol. III, p 551.
[495] Rawlins to Emma, March 30, 1869 in Wilson, *Rawlins*, 355.
[496] Wilson, *Rawlins*, 376.
[497] Ibid., 358.
[498] Smith, 496.
[499] Ibid., 376.
[500] Cox, 165.
[501] Cox, 164.
[502] Letters sent by Sec. War 1800-1889, roll 60, Vol 63-64. LC.
[503] Smith, 493.
[504] Marti, Jose, *The America of Jose Marti*, N.Y.: Noonday, 1953, 13.
[505] Ibid., 48.
[506] *New York Herald*, Sept. 1, Sept. 8, 1869.
[507] Ely Parker, in Wilson, *Rawlins*, 502.
[508] Wilson, *Rawlins*, 368.
[509] Rawlins was moved there because there was no one living in his home. Cadwallader had lived with him in the Georgetown home until his wife arrived in Washington. Cadwallader had a son whom he named Rawlins.
[510] Green, 283.
[511] Armstrong, 173.
[512] *Galena Gazette*, Sept. 17, 1869.
[513] *New York Herald*, September 8, 1869, quoted in McFeely, 330.

[514] McFeely, 330.
[515] *Galena Evening Gazette*, September 7, 1869.
[516] Smith, 688 n. 6.
[517] Cox, Jacob Dolson, "How Judge Hoar Ceased to be Attorney-General," *Atlantic Monthly*, 76:164 (August 1895).
[518] Nevins, vol.1, 247; Smith, 688 n. 17.
[519] Logan, 206.
[520] Smith, 688 n. 6.
[521] Widow application 214628; certificate 134796; minor benefits 610013; certificate 442479, NA.
[522] A Galena physician, later on Grant's staff.
[523] Widow's Brief # 2, October 14, 1874; Affidavit of Edw. Kittoe, August 21, 1874, NA.
[524] Box 3377, National Archives, Cert. 167.018.
[525] *Danbury News-Times,* July 24, 1894.
[526] *Evening Star*, May 30, 1872.
[527] *Independent Republican* (Goshen), January 23, 1917.
[528] Robert J., James S., William D., Lemuel D., and Laura.
[529] *Galena Weekly*, July13, 1893.
[530] McFeely, 435.
[531] Babcock was acquitted through Grant's intercession.
[532] Porter, Horace, "General Ulysses S. Grant," p. 369 in *Personal Recollections of the War,* ed. J. G. Wilson and T. M. Coan, Series I, N.Y.: Loyal Legion, 1891.
[533] Groom, 448.
[534] Waugh, 264.

BIBLIOGRAPHY

Anderson, Nancy Scott, and Anderson, Dwight. *The General*. N.Y.: Knopf, 1987.

Armstrong, William. *Warrior in Two Camps.* Syracuse: Syracuse University Press, 1978.

Badeau, Adam. *Military History of Ulysses S. Grant*. N.Y.: Appleton, 1868.

Battles and Leaders of the Civil War, 4 vol. Secaucus, N.J.: Castle, 2000.

Beale, H. K. and Brownsword, A. W. [editors]. *Diary of Gideon Wells*. N.Y.: Norton, 3 vol.

Bonekemper III, Edward H. *A Victor not a Butcher*. Washington: Regnery (Eagle), 2004.

Brinton, John H. *The Personal Memoirs of John H. Brinton*. N.Y.: Neale, 1914.

Buell, Thomas B. *The Warrior Generals Combat Leadership*. N.Y.: Three Rivers, 1993.

Bunting III, Josiah. *Ulysses S. Grant*. N.Y.: Holt, 2004.

Burne, Alfred H. *Lee, Grant and Sherman.* N.Y.: Scribner, 1939.

Butler, Benjamin F. *Butler's Book.* Boston: Thayer, 1892.

Cadwallader, Sylvanus. *Three Years with Grant.* N.Y.: Knopf, 1955.

Catton, Bruce. *Grant Moves South.* Boston: Little Brown, 1960

Catton, Bruce. *Grant Takes Command.* Boston: Little Brown, 1968

Chetlain, Augustus. *Recollections of Seventy Years.* Galena: Gazette Publications, 1899.

Conger, A. L. *Rise of US Grant.* N.Y.: Century, 1931.

Cox, Jacob D. "How Judge Hoar Ceased to be Attorney-General." *Atlantic Monthly* 76, (Aug. 1895).

Cox, Jacob D. *Military Reminiscences of the Civil War*, 2 vol. N.H.: Scribner, 1900.

Crozier, Emmet. *Yankee Reporter 1861-65.* N.Y.: Oxford, 1956.

Dana, Charles A. *Recollections of the Civil War.* N.Y.: Appleton, 1898

Daniel, Larry. *Shiloh,* N.Y.: Simon and Schuster, 1997

Donald, David. *Charles Sumner and the Rights of Man*. N.Y.: Knopf, 1970.

Drake, Rebecca Blackwell. "Union Headquarters." http//battleofraymond.org history/lum htm.

Eisenschiml, Otto, and Newman, Ralph. *The Civil War*. Secaucus: Blue and Grey, 1956.

Emerson, John W. "Grant's Life in the West." *Midland Monthly*, Vol. IX, Jan. 1898, Jan-April.

Flood, Charles B. *Grant and Sherman*. N.Y.: Farrar, Straus, Giroux, 2005.

Foote, Shelby. *The Civil War*, 3 vol. N.Y.: Random House Vintage, 1986.

Frost, Jashine C. *Ancestors of Hiram Smith and his wife Sarah Jane Bull*. N.Y. 1927 private printing in *http://longeland* genealogy.com/Smith Bull.pdf.

Furgurson, Ernest B. *Not War But Murder*. N.Y.: Knopf, 2000.

"Glimpses of the Nations Struggle" (Military Order Vol. 3).

Grant, Julia Dent. *The Personal Memoirs of Julia Dent Grant*. N.Y.: Putnam, 1975.

Grant, Susan-Mary and Reid, Brian. *The Civil War*. N.Y.: Longman, 2000.

Grant, Ulysses S. *Personal Memoirs, two vol. in one.* N.Y.: Webster, 1894.

Grant, Ulysses S. *Memoirs and Selected Letters.* N.Y.: Carbondale: Southern Illinois University Press, 1975.

Grant, U.S. *Papers of Ulysses S. Grant* [edited by John Y. Simon]. Carbondale: Southern Illinois University Press, 1967-2007.

Green, Horace. *General Grant's Last Stand.* N.Y.: Scribner, 1936.

Greenbie, Majorie Barstow. *My Dear Lady.* N.Y.: Arno, 1974.

Griffith, Paddy. *Battle Tactics of the Civil War.* New Haven: Yale University Press, 2001.

Groom, Winston. *Vicksburg 1863.* N.Y.: Knopf, 2009.

Howard, O. O. and Parker E. "Some Reminiscences of Grant." *McClure Magazine*, May 1894.

Hughes, Jr., and Nathaniel Cheairs. *The Battle of Belmont.* Chapel Hill: University North Carolina, 1991.

Hurd, D. Hamilton. *History of Fairfield County, Connecticut.* Philadelphia: Lewis, 1881.

Hurst, Jack. *Men of Fire.* N.Y.: Perseus, 2007.

Jenney, William. *Personal Recollections of Vicksburg*, Vol. III. 1899.

Jewett, E. Funeral Discourse of Rev. Dr. Jewett at Galena on Sept. 19, 1869.

Jordan, David M. *Winfield Scott Hancock*. Bloomington, Ind.: Indiana University Press, 1988.

Kelsey, Marie Ellen. *Ulysses S. Grant: A Biography*. Praeger, 2005.

Korda, Michael. *Ulysses S. Grant The Unlikely Hero*. N.Y.: Harper Collins, 2004.

Korn, Bertram. *American Jewry and the Civil War*. Philadelphia: Jewish Publication Society, 2001.

Lewis, Lloyd. *Captain Sam Grant*. Boston: Little Brown, 1950.

Lincoln, Abraham. *Collected Works* [edited by Nicolay and Hay]. Harrogate, Tenn.: Lincoln Memorial University, 1894.

Logan, Mary. *Reminiscences of the Civil War and Reconstruction*. Carbondale, Ill: Southern Illinois University Press, 1970

Longacre, Edward G. *General Ulysses S. Grant*. N.Y.: Da Capo, 2006.

Lyman, Theodore. *Meade's Headquarters*. Boston: *Atlantic Monthly*, 1922.

Macartney, Clarence E. *Grant and His Generals.* N.Y.: McBride, 1953.

McDonough, James Lee. *Shiloh.* Knoxville: University of Tennessee Press, 1977.

Mc Feely, William S. *Grant.* N.Y.: Norton, 1981.

Mc Feely, Mary D and William S. [editors]. *Ulysses S. Grant Memoirs and Selected Letters.* Library of America, 1990.

McPherson, James. *Battle Cry of Freedom.* N.Y.: Oxford, 1988.

Marshall-Cornwall, Gen. Sir James. *Grant as Military Commander.* NY: Van Nostrand Reinhold, 1970.

Marszalek, John F. *Sherman.* N.Y.: Free Press, 1993.

Marszalek, John F. *Commander of All Lincoln's Armies.* Cambridge, Mass.: Harvard University Press, 2004.

Marti, Jose. *The America of Jose Marti.* N.Y.: Noonday, 1953.

Miers, Earl Schenck. *The Web of Victory.* N.Y.: Knopf, 1955.

National Archives: Union Staff Officers file 1861-65; Secretary War files under Pres. Grant; Medical Records; Pension Files.

Nevins, Allan. *Hamilton Fish*, 2 vol. N.Y.: Ungar, 1967.

Parker, Arthur C. *Life of General Ely S. Parker*. Buffalo, N.Y.: Buffalo Hist. Soc., Vol. VIII, 1919; http://www.archiv.org/details/life of general

Parker, Arthur Coswell. *The Life of Ely S. Parker*. Buffalo: Buffalo Historical Society, 1919.

Parker, Ely S. The Character of Grant, in *Personal Recollections of the War of the Rebellion*, edited by James Grant Wilson and Tilas M. Coan. N.Y.: Commandery Military Order of the Loyal Legion of the U.S., 1891 Series 1.

Perret, Geoffrey. *Ulysses S. Grant*. N.Y.: Random, 1997.

Personal Recollections of the war of the Rebellion, edited by James Grant Wilson and Tilas M. Coan. N.Y.: Commandery Military Order of the Loyal Legion of the U.S., 1891 Series 1

Porter, Horace. "General Ulysses S. Grant", in the *Personal Recollections of the War of the Rebellion*, edited by James Grant Wilson and Tilas M. Coan. N.Y.: Commandery Military Order of the Loyal Legion of the U.S., 1891 Series 1

Porter, Horace. *Campaigning with Grant*. N.Y.: Da Capo, 1986.

Reeder, Red. *The Northern Generals*. N.Y.: Duell, Sloan and Pearce, 1964.

Reid, Brian H., Grant, Susan-Mary. *The Civil War*. N.Y.: Longman, 2000.

Rhea, Gordon C. *The Battle of the Wilderness*. Baton Rouge: Louisiana State University, 1995.

Rhea, Gordon C. *Cold Harbor*. Baton Rouge: Louisiana State University, 2002.

Richardson, Albert D. *A Personal History of Ulysses S. Grant*. Boston: Guernsey, 1885.

Santovenia y Eshaide, Emelerio. *John A. Rawlins*. Habana: El Siglo XX, 1931.

Schofield, John M. *Forty Six Years in the Army*. N.Y.: Century, 1897.

Schutz, Duane. *The Most Glorious Fourth*. Vicksburg and Gettysburg, N.Y.: Norton, 2002.

Shannon, Fred Albert. *The Organization and Administration of the Union Army, 1861-1865*. Cleveland: Clark, 1928.

Shaw, John. "The Life and Services of General John A. Rawlins." *Glimpses of the Nations Struggle*, Vol. III, 387.

Sheridan, Philip H. *Personal Memoirs of P. H. Sheridan*, Vol. 1. N.Y.: Webster, 1888.

Sherman, Hoyt. "Personal Recollections of General Grant." *Midland Monthly*, April-December, 1898.

Simpson, Brooks. *Let us Have Peace*. Chapel Hill: University of North Carolina, 1991.

Simpson, Brooks D. *Ulysses S. Grant*. Boston: Houghton Mifflin, 2000.

Smith, Jean Edward. *Grant*. N.Y.: Simon and Schuster, 2001.

Smith, John C. *Personal Recollections of General Ulysses S. Grant*. Self published, Feb. 11, 1904.

Temple, Oliver P. *East Tennessee and the Civil War*. Cincinnati: Clark, 1899.

Trudeau, Noah. *Bloody Roads South*. Boston: Little, Brown, 1989.

Walker, Peter R. *Vicksburg*. Chapel Hill: University of North Carolina, 1960.

Wallace, Lew. *Lew Wallace: An Autobiography*. N.Y.: Harpers and Brothers, 1906.

Walsh, George. *Whip the Rebellion*. N.Y.: Tom Doherty, 2005.

War of the Rebellion, A Compilation of the Official Records of the Union and Confederate Armies, 130 vol. Washington, D.C.: Government Printing Office, 1880-1901.

Waugh, Joan. *Ulysses S. Grant.* Chapel Hill: University of North Carolina, 2009.

Wells, Gideon. *Diary of Gideon Wells*, 3 vol. N.Y.: Norton, 1960.

Williams, John H. *A Great and Shining Road.* Lincoln, Neb: University of Nebraska, 1988.

Williams, Kenneth P. *Lincoln Finds a General.* N.Y.: Macmillan 5 vol., 1952.

Williams, T. Harry. *Lincoln and His Generals.* N.Y.: Random House Vintage, 1952.

Wilson, J. H. *The Life of Charles H. Dana.* N.Y.: Harper, 1907.

Wilson, James H. *Life of John A. Rawlins.* N.Y.: Neale, 1916

Wilson, Lynn W. *History of Fairfield County Connecticut.* Chicago: Clarke, 1929.

Wittley, Charles. *War Memoranda.* Cleveland: William and William, 1884.

Woodman, Harold D. *King Cotton and his Retainers*, Washington, D.C.: Beard, 2000.

Woodward, W. E. *Meet General Grant.* N.Y.: Liveright, 1928.

Woodworth, Steven E. *Nothing But Victory.* N.Y.: Knopf, 2005.

NEWSPAPERS AND MAGAZINES

Army and Navy Journal, Sept. 12, 1868.

Chicago Tribune, 4/17/1892.

Danbury News-Times, July 24, 1994.

Danbury Times, December 22, 1863; Sept 11, 17, 21 1869.

Galena Evening Gazette, September 7, 8, 11, 17, 21 1869.

Galena Weekly, July 1893.

Goshen Democrat, 9/6/82; 9/7/1982.

Goshen Independent Republican, 9/9/1869; 9/6/1882; 1/23/1917.

Harper's New Monthly Magazine, May 1866.

Harper's Weekly, 12/10/64.

INDEX

Alcohol dependence, Moral stigma, viii
Amelia Court House, 186, 187
Amphictyonic Society, 6
Antrobus, John, painted a portrait of Rawlins, 175
Appomattox Court House, 186
   Surrender, 189, 197
Appomattox Court House Station, 187
Appomattox River, 153
Arizona Territory, 207
Arkansas Post (Fort Hindman), 69
Army discipline, 94
Army of the Cumberland, 60, 103, 108, 111, 132
   Trapped at Chattanooga, 108
Army of the James, 132, 141, 144, 158
Army of the Ohio, 51, 59, 132
Army of the Potomac, 124, 126, 128, 129, 130, 132, Army of the Potomac (Cont.) 133, 141, 146, 149, 154, 155, 164, 165, 178, 182, 186
Army of the Tennessee, 51, 58, 126, 132, 197
Army of the Virginia, 128
Army resignations, 17
Atlanta, 170, 174
Babcock, Orville E, 127, 156, 164, 166, 199, 204, 206, 217
   scandal, 219
Back pay grab scandal, 219
Badeau, Adam, 88, 126, 176, 181, 206
   photo, 153
Bailly, Joseph A, sculptor of Rawlins statue, 215
Banks, Nathaniel, 81, 93, 104, 105, 127, 128, 131
Barnes, Bill, Grant's servant, 35, 88
Baton Rouge LA, 79
Battle above the Clouds (Lookout Mountain), 115
Belknap, William W, 219

Belknap Indian agent bribery scandal, 219
Belmont MO, Battle of, 33, 34
  Map, 33
Benedict, Nathan, 119
Bennett, James Gordon, 210
Bermuda Hundred, 141, 146, 150, 153, 183
Bertram, Bernice, x
Big Black River, 84
Black Hawk War, 2, 22
"Black Republican Meeting", 13
Black troops, Recruitment, 104
Blikenderfer, Jacob, 202
Bliss, D W, 212
Booth, John Wilkes, 88
Boston MA, 194
Boutwell, George, 206
Bowers, Theodore S (Joe), 135, 145, 156, 163, 164, 165, 178, 194
  Joe, 119, 186, 195
  Joseph, 126
  T S, 47, 66, 76, 86, 101, 121
Boydton Plank Road, 154, 165, 166, 169, 170, 181, 184
Bragg, Braxton, 115
Bridgeport TN, 108, 112
Brinton, Dr John, 42
  appreciation of Rawlins, ix
  ordered not to dispense alcohol to staff, 31
Brock Road, 134
Brooklyn Bridge, 212
Brown's Ferry, 111
Bruinsburg, 81
Buell, Don Carlos, 47, 48, 51, 52, 53, 54, 59, 60
  late arrival at Pittsburg Landing, 56
Burgess Mill VA, 169
Burlington NJ, 176, 190
Burnside, Ambrose, 133
  at battle of the Wilderness, 136
  at Petersburg, 162
Butler, Benjamin, 127, 132, 141, 158, 159, 168
  dismissed, 179
Cadwallader, Sylvanus, viii, 84, 89, 92, 96, 117, 172, 173, 178, 179, 195, 196, 206, 221
  account of Satartia drinking binge, 90, 91, 93
  reporter and Freemason, 60
Cairo IL, 38, 107
California Gold Rush, 2
Canals, 72
Cedar Creek VA, 169, 174
Censorship, 49
Chagres River, Panama, 16
Chambersburg PA, Burned by Early, 158, 163
Champion Hill, Fierce battle, 83, 84, 87

Charcoal, Importance to lead smelting, 4
Charcoal burning
  Process described, 4, 5
  Rawlins family livelihood, 3, 5
Charleston Harbor, 12
Chase, Salmon P, 62
Chattahoochee River, 159
Chattanooga TN, 106, 107, 108, 109, 110, 115, 216
  Battle of, 111, 112
    map, 111
  Battle report, 121
  Important rail center, 103, 104
Cheyenne WT, 202, 217
Chicago IL, 195, 202
Chickahominy River, 145
Chickamauga, 159
  Battle of, 106, 107
Chickasaw Bayou, 71, 85, 92
Chickasaw Bluff, 92
Cholera, Strikes Grant's regiment in Panama, 17
Cincinnati OH, 198
City Point, 152, 161, 167, 172, 176, 178, 180, 185, 186, 188, 189
  Explosion on ammunition barge, 164
Civil Rights Act of 1875, 219
Cleveland OH, 196
Climate, Southern, 87, 88, 156

Cold Harbor VA, Battle of, 146, 149, 150, 151, 152
Collier, Lovisa, 1, 2
Columbia SC, Burned, 181
Columbus KY, 33, 34
  Capture and fortification by Confederates, 29
  Strategic port on Mississippi River, 28
Compromise of 1850, 13
Comstock, Cyrus B, 102, 125, 126, 128, 176
  at Battle of Cold Harbor, 147, 148
Confederate Army of Tennessee, 132
Continental Divide, 203
Corinth MS, 53, 54, 56, 58
  Important Confederate rail center, 51
Corruption in Grant's quartermaster department, 37, 38
Cotton, Economic issues, 62, 63
Covington KY, 42, 50
Cox, Jacob D, 206, 213, 214
Cruces, Panama, 16
Cuba, 201, 210, 211, 213
Culpepper Court House VA, 128
Cumberland River, 40, 44
  Strategic importance, 28
Dana, viii
  Charles A, 63, 78, 81, 84, 85, 90, 93, 100, 108, 113,

Charles A, (Cont.)
  123, 127, 148, 157, 161,
  167, 210, 221
  account of Satartia
    drinking binge, 89
  journalist, 74
Danbury CT, 105, 118, 119,
  167, 176, 186, 194, 198,
  207, 211, 217
Daniels
  Charles F, 217
  Mary Emmelene (Emma)
    Rawlins, 217
Danville Line, 187
Davis, Jefferson, 81, 104,
  159
  captured by Wilson, 190
Dent
  Frederick, 127, 156
  John D, 219
  Julia, 14, 16, 19, 23, 24,
    30, 36, 42, 50, 64, 65, 68,
    78, 81, 96, 97, 103, 105,
    107, 114, 118, 120, 121,
    126, 132, 167, 175, 180,
    186, 189, 194, 213, 219,
    221
    joins Ulysses in
      Memphis, 58
    owned 2 slaves, 18
    returns to St Louis, 59
    with Ulysses in Corinth,
      59
Department of Tennessee, 58
Department of the
  Mississippi, 108

Desertions, 74, 183
Detroit MI, 196
  Grant posted at, 16
Diligent, Boat to Satartia, 91,
  92
Dinwiddie Court House, 184
Disease among troops, 74
Dodge
  G M, 200, 203, 207
  Grenville, 202
Donelson, Andrew Jackson,
  119
Douglas
  John Hancock, 212
  John M, 7
  Stephen A, 10, 195
Douglas Democrats, 11
Draft Exemption, 154, 155
Drewry's Bluff, 141
Drinking, Among Grant's
  staff, 31
Duff, William L, 73, 75, 84,
  118, 126, 140, 156
  criticized by Dana, 85
Dunn
  William McKee Jr, 168
Dunn, William M, 127, 200,
  202
Early, Jubal, 152, 157, 162,
  169
  terrorizes Maryland, 158,
    163
Eaton, John, 61
Enlistment Bounty, 155
Enlistments, Expiration, 130,
  144, 165

Erie Canal, 20
False allegations of Grant's drunkenness, 38, 39
Farragut, Adm, 195, 196
Fish, Hamilton, 206, 210, 211, 215
Fisher Hill VA, 169
Five Forks, 184, 185
Foote, Andrew H, 28, 39, 40
Ford's Theater, 190
Fort Donelson, 40, 44, 45
   Appalling conditions, 48
   Captured by Grant, 46
      promotions of Grant, McClernand and Rawlins, 49
Fort Fisher, Captured by Union troops, 179
Fort Henry, 40, 41
   Captured by Grant, 43
Fort Henry-Fort Donelson, Map, 43
Fort Lafayette NY, 67
Fort Monroe, 132
Fort Pemberton, 73
Fort Stedman, 183
Fort Sumter SC, 12
Fort Vancouver OT, 21
Fourteenth Amendment, 198
Fox tribe, 2
Franklin TN, Battle of, 177
Frederick MD, Ransomed, 152
Freemasons, 7, 20, 84, 99
Fremont, John C, 22, 32, 37, 86

French Broad River, 119
French troops in Mexico, 131
Fuller, Allen C, 11
Galena Academy, 5
Galena IL, x, 1, 2, 7, 9, 10, 12, 20, 164, 194, 200, 201, 205
   Center of lead mining industry, 3
   Important commercial center by 1855, 4
Galena River, 1
Ganley, Mrs Jean, x
Georgetown Heights, 212, 217
Gettysburg PA, 159
   Won the same day as Vicksburg, 93
Globe Tavern Station, 165
Gold scandal, 219
Goshen NY, 8, 23
Grand Gulf MS, 79, 80, 81
Grand Junction TN, Site of contraband camp for displaced black population, 61
Grant
   Fred, 78, 80, 81, 120, 125
      injured in battle of Champion Hill, 84
      son of Ulysses S, 22
   Hannah, 50
      mother of Ulysses S, 21
   Jesse, 24, 42, 50, 63, 180
      father of Ulysses S, 14,

father of Ulysses S (Cont.) 18
  a fierce abolitionist, 18
  a Freemason, 20
  son of Ulysses S, 68, 105, 107, 126
  successful merchant, 18
Julia (Dent), 16, 19, 23, 24, 30, 36, 42, 50, 58, 64, 65, 68, 78, 81, 96, 97, 103, 105, 107, 114, 118, 120, 121, 126, 132, 175, 180, 186, 189, 194, 213, 219, 221
  owned 2 slaves, 18
  returns to St Louis, 59
  with Ulysses in Corinth, 59
Noah, grandfather of Ulysses, 18
Orville, 24, 219
  brother of Ulysses, 18
  a Freemason, 20
Simpson
  brother of Ulysses, 18, 166
  a Freemason, 20
  lived with Ulysses' family, 19
  ran Jesse's store, 18
  suffered from terminal consumption, 18
Ulysses Jr (Buck), 78, 81
Ulysses S, vii, viii, ix, 14, 15, 22, 24, 33, 36, 40, 51,

Ulysses S (Cont.)
55, 65, 67, 68, 69, 70, 72, 74, 75, 76, 77, 78, 80, 81, 83, 84, 85, 86, 87, 88, 93, 94, 95, 97, 98, 100, 101, 102, 107, 108, 115, 116, 117, 118, 120, 121, 122, 123, 125, 128, 129, 130, 131, 132, 133, 138, 139, 140, 141, 142, 143, 144, 145, 146, 150, 154, 155, 156, 157, 159, 160, 161, 162, 165, 167, 169, 171, 172, 173, 175, 176, 177, 178, 179, 181, 182, 183, 185, 188, 189, 190, 193, 194, 195, 196, 197, 198, 199, 200, 201, 203, 207, 208, 209, 211, 212, 214, 215, 217, 218, 221, 222
  administration plagued by scandals, 219
  administration's redeeming features, 219
  alcohol affliction, viii, 88, 89
  asks Lee for surrender, 187
  attempts to halt illicit cotton trade, 103
  at Battle of Belmont MO, 34
  at Battle of Cold Harbor, 147, 148, 149

at battle of the Wilderness, 135, 136, 137
begins drinking in Mexico, 16
business ventures on Pacific coast, 17
at Cairo MO, 27, 28, 29
called to Washington, 124
clerk in father's store, 19
death from throat cancer, 221
death from throat cancer described, 90
fallen upon by horse, 105, 109
family issues, 18
first child born, 16
at Fort Donelson, 46
grandfather Noah a Rev War veteran and drunkard, 18
headquarters in Memphis, 58
headquarters in Nashville, 119
health problems, 166
heavy drinking during Pacific service, 17
his staff officers in Washington, 126, 127
humiliated by Halleck after Pittsburg Landing, 57
Inauguration, 206
journey over Isthmus of Panama, 16
left Fort Donelson without permission, 48
meets with George Thomas at Chattanooga, 110
in Mexican War, 15
at Mexico City, 15
at Monterrey, 15
and Native American (Know Nothing) Party, 63
nominated for presidency, 204, 205
opposed cotton trade, 62
ordered to return to Fort Donelson, 48
photo, 153
at Pittsburg Landing, 53, 54
posted to West Coast, 16
public image, viii
reinforces army with troops from Washington, 145
reports of drunkenness, 61
rushes to Rawlins' deathbed, 213
at Sacketts Harbor NY, 16
at Saint Louis MO, 14, 16, 17

sends Sheridan after
  Early, 163
service on Isthmus of
  Panama, 17
supports efforts to enlist
  Black soldiers, 61
tomb, 221
trip to New Orleans, 104
trip to Satartia, 91, 92
weakness in staff
  organization, 46
at West Point, 14
wife Julia owned 2
  slaves, 18
wrote his own orders, 82
Greeley, Horace, 74, 216
Greenbacks, 152
Grenada MS, 68
Grierson, William, 79
Guilford IL, 2, 9, 213
Gunboats, 37
Haines Bluff, 91
Halleck, Henry W, 32, 41,
  48, 50, 53, 57, 58, 66, 67,
  87, 104, 122, 131, 139, 140,
  165, 174, 175
  military career, 40
  suspends Grant, 48
Hallet, Mr, 5
Hammer, Gen Tom, 15
Hancock, Winfield Scott, 199
Hanover Town VA, 145
Hard Times, 79, 80
Harvard, 182
Hatcher's Run, 181

Hawkins, Capt, 47
Haynes Bluff, 79
Hekadelphoi Society, 6
Hillyer
  Mrs, 36, 65
  William S, 35, 38, 47, 54, 102
    heavy drinker, 30
Hilton Head NC, 71
Hoar, Senator, 159
Holly Springs MS, 64
  Destruction of rail line, 68
Holman
  George W, 218
  Jennie, 218
  Jennie (Rawlins), 218
Hood, John Bell, 159, 170, 172, 173, 174, 176, 177
  abandons Atlanta, 160
  defeated by Thomas near
    Nashville, 178
  moves north after
    abandoning Atlanta, 170
Hooker, Joseph, 108, 111, 115, 121, 133
Hornets Nest, 55
Horses, 42, 43, 81, 92, 177
  In battle, 34, 35
  Cincinnati, 137
  General Blair, 137
  "Jeff Davis", 206
  Sheridan's "Rienzi", 169
Howard, Oliver O, 108
Hudson, Peter, 127
Hunter, 152

Hurlburt
  Mary Emmelene (Emma), 96, 97, 98, 106, 107, 114, 118
  Sarah (Pret), 119
  Stephen Ambler, 119
Illinois Central Railroad, 7
Isthmus of Panama, 16
J R Grant & Sons, 20, 24
Jablonsky, Elsa, x
Jackson
  Andrew, 119
  Stonewall, 152
Jackson MS, 82
  Military stores captured, 83
James River, 132, 149, 152, 153, 166, 182
Jerusalem Plank Road, 154, 155, 177
Jews
  Expelled from Grant's department, 64
  In Memphis, 64
  In Memphis region implicated by Grant in cotton trade, 63
  Officers tendered resignations, 64
Jo Daviess County IL, 1, 5
  Leading lead producing county in US, 4
Johnson
  Andrew, 195, 196, 198, 199, 200, 202, 204, 206, 219
  Lyndon, 219
Johnston
  Albert Sidney, 52
  Joseph E, 82, 132, 156, 157, 183, 186, 190
    defeated at Jackson MS, 83
    relieved of duty, 159
Jones, J Russell, 12, 63, 123, 127, 175, 201, 206
Juarez, Benito, Mexican president, 131
Kansas-Nebraska Act, 13
Kansas-Nebraska Bill, 10
Kenesaw Mountain, Battle of, 157
Kentucky, Strategic importance and divided loyalty, 28
King of Spades, Nickname for Robert E Lee, 142
Kittoe, Edward D, 216
Koch, Robert, 23
La Grange TN, 65
  Grant's headquarters, 64
Lagow
  Clark B, 47, 76, 80, 103, 113
   heavy drinker, 30
Lake Ontario, 16
Lake Providence, 72
"Lead mine district," northwest Illinois, 1
"Lead Mine Regiment", 23
Lee
  Mrs Mary, 20

Robert E, 40, 87, 126, 129, 133, 134, 138, 139, 142, 143, 144, 150, 152, 162, 163, 166, 167, 181, 183, 185, 186, 187, 188, 189, 190, 193, 196, 197
  at Battle of Cold Harbor, 147
  at battle of the Wilderness, 135
Leet, George K, 102, 119, 126, 164, 194
Lincoln, Abraham, 10, 12, 24, 34, 36, 40, 61, 66, 78, 85, 87, 98, 99, 108, 123, 127, 128, 154, 160, 168, 172, 174, 177, 190, 219
  frantic request for troops to defend Washington, 157
  sends for Grant, 158
Lincoln, Robert, 182
  son of President, 181
Lincoln-Douglas Debate, 10
Logan, John, 22, 67, 177, 210, 215
Longstreet, James, 104
Lookout Mountain, 106, 110, 122
  Battle of, 115
Louisville KY, 107, 108, 120
Lum
  Anna Maria, 96
  William, 96
Lynchburg VA, 150, 152, 186
Lyons, Nathaniel, 22
Mack
  Harmon, 63
  Henry, 63
Magnolia, Headquarters ship, 74, 77, 78
Marti, Jose, 201, 211
Maximilian
  Archduke, 131
  Emperor, 193
McClellan, George, 21, 40, 48
McClernand, John A, 22, 34, 35, 36, 38, 45, 46, 64, 65, 66, 67, 69, 77, 79, 80, 81, 85, 86, 98, 99
  supports Rawlins and Grant, 48
  suspended by Grant, 87
McPherson, James B, 47, 53, 54, 55, 59, 60, 65, 75, 78, 79, 86, 124, 126, 132, 221
  death, 160
  early career, 42
  Grant's staff engineer, 42
Meade, George, 128, 129, 130, 132, 133, 138, 141, 144, 149, 158, 162, 183
  at Battle of Cold Harbor, 148
  at battle of the Wilderness, 135, 136
Mexican War, 15, 21, 22, 40
Mexico, 193
Mexico City, 15
Miineral Point WI, 2

Milliken's Bend, 70, 79
Miners Lodge No. 273, 7
Missionary Ridge, 110, 115
  Battle of, 116
    enhanced Grant's reputation, 117
Mississippi River, 73, 85
  Impediments removed at last, 93
  Union forces set to remove Confederate obstacles, 66
Mobile AL, 131, 190
Mobile Bay, 174
Monocacy River, 157
Monterrey, 15
Mt Morris IL, 5
Mule Shoe, 138, 139, 140
Nashville TN, 47, 120, 121, 170, 177, 178
  Grant's headquarters, 119
Natchez, 73
National Convention of Soldiers and Sailors, 204
Native American (Know Nothing) Party, 63
Nevins, Allan, 215
New Carthage LA, 79
New Orleans LA, 66, 104, 105
New York NY, 194
North Anna River, 143, 144
North Carolina, 190
North Fork, 82
Omaha NE, 202
Ord, 221
  E O, 158

Edward, 87
Order #11 (Jewish expulsion from Grant's department),
  Cancelled by Lincoln, 64
Overland Campaign, 133
  Casualties, 149
Paducah KY, 33, 41, 86
  Jews forced to leave, 64
  Occupied by Grant, 29
Pamunkey River, 144
Panama City, Panama, 16
Panama Railroad, 16
Parker, Ely S, 7, 20, 76, 95, 99, 100, 101, 109, 119, 126, 135, 164, 168, 186, 194, 195, 207, 212, 220
  a Freemason, 20
  photo, 95
  a Seneca Indian, 19
Pasini, Steve, x
Pasteur, Louis, 23
Peace vs Surrender, 188
Peebles Farm, 166
Pemberton, John C, 82, 84, 96
Petersburg Campaign, 154, 158, 160
  Gigantic explosion, 162
  Map, 155
  Records, 194
  Union debacle, 162
Petersburg VA, 130, 132, 141, 149, 165, 167, 170, 177, 181, 182, 183, 185, 186, 187

Enemy entrenchments, 153
Important rail center, 150
Investment continued 10 months, 151
Philadelphia PA, 194
Phillipsburg NY, 218
Pittsburg Landing (Shiloh), 57
  Appalling losses on both sides, 56
  Battle of, 52
    map, 52
  Grant's unpreparedness, 56
Polk, Leonidas, 29, 32, 33, 35
Port Gibson, 82
Port Hudson LA, 66, 73, 88, 93
Porter, 82, 171, 181, 199, 206
  Adm, 72
  David, 179, 215
  Flag Officer, 73
  Horace, 127
Potomac River, 157
Pret, Sarah, 119
Price, Sterling, 175
Prisoners, northern, 67
Prisoners, Taken at Vicksburg, 93
Provisions, Shortages, 187
Public opinion, Turns against Grant during Vicksburg Campaign, 74

Raccoon Mountain, 109
Radical Republican Party, 201
Rapidan River, 133, 144
Rawlins, 117
  Emily, 218
    daughter of John A Rawlins, 9, 106
  Emily (Smith), 8, 9, 180, 217
    death, 23
    photo, 8
  James, 218
    son of John A Rawlins, 9
  James Bradner, 218
  James Dawson, 2, 3
    father of John A Rawlins, 1
  Jane Louisa ("Jennie"), 9
  Jarrard Owen, 3
  Jennie, 218
    daughter of John A Rawlins, 180
  John A, vii, viii, ix, 3, 8, 9, 10, 21, 23, 24, 36, 38, 41, 47, 55, 57, 59, 65, 66, 67, 71, 72, 78, 81, 82, 83, 84, 85, 86, 88, 91, 92, 93, 94, 97, 100, 101, 103, 104, 109, 110, 116, 122, 123, 124, 126, 127, 128, 132, 133, 137, 140, 141, 142, 146, 149, 156, 157, 158, 160, 162, 163, 164, 165, 166, 167, 168, 171, 172,

John A (Cont.)
173, 176, 178, 179, 182, 185, 188, 189, 191, 193, 194, 195, 196, 197, 198, 204, 205, 207, 210, 213, 215, 217, 219
  adamantly prohibited liquor at headquarters, 39, 40
  at Battle of Belmont MO, 35
  at Battle of Cold Harbor, 147, 148
  at battle of the Wilderness, 135, 136
  begins duties as Grant's Assistant Adjutant General (AAD), 29, 30
  begins law career, 7
  body moved to Arlington National Cemetery, 215
  courtship of Emma Hurlburt, 105
  debates with Fuller, 11
  declining health, 199, 200, 202, 209, 211, 212
  defends Grant after Fort Donelson, 48
  as described by Dana, 75, 76, 77
  destroys alcohol in staff tents, 89
  dismal financial situation, 201
  education, 5, 6
  and Emma's 3 infants died, 120
  a Freemason, 20
  friendly relations with the press, 41, 60
  funeral, 213, 214
  gifted orator, 6
  goes to Washington, 99
  good friends with McPherson, 42
  good memory, 5
  habit of cursing, 77
  law practice expands, 9
  letters to Emma, 107, 112, 114, 115, 120, 125, 129, 130, 139, 144, 145, 152, 154, 159, 161, 175, 186
  marries Mary Emmeline Hurlburt, 119
  moral supervision of Grant in Julia's absence, 50
  obtains written promise from Grant to abstain from drinking, 30, 39
  offers to resign, 125
  persistent cough, 118, 130, 145
  photo, 95, facing page 125, 153, 180
  photo of statue, 222
  at Pittsburg Landing, 53, 54
  plans to marry, 118

praises Smith's black troops, 151
protests Grants Order #11, 64
reports to Nashville with wife and children, 120
requests medical leave, 118
reviews Chattanooga battle report, 121
as Secretary of War, 208
speaks against rebellious South, 13
statue commissioned, 215
"the Coal Boy", 5
threatens to resign due to Grant's drinking, 89
tour of the West, 203
well liked and respected by staff officers, 50
wished to purge drinkers from Grant's staff, 102
John A (Black John), 95
John Aaron, 2
Julia (Dent), 167
Laura, 67
Lovisa, 218
Lovisa (Collier), 1, 2
Mary, died in infancy, 217
Mary Emmelene (Emma), 175, 186, 189, 194, 200, 212, 216, 217
  notified of John's death, 213
Mary Emmelene (Emma) (Hurlburt), 98
Mary Lovisa ("Laura"), 5
Violet, died in infancy, 217
Willie
  died in infancy, 217
  infant son of John A, 200
Rawlins Park, 216
  Washington DC, 222
Rawlins WY, 203
Reame's Station, 165
Reconstruction, 195
Red River, 131
Repp, Steve, x
Richmond Campaign, Records, 194
Richmond VA, 130, 137, 138, 139, 141, 144, 145, 146, 149, 150, 153, 182
Richmond-Danville Railroad, 186
Rifles
  Enfield, 87
  Spencer repeating, 146
  Springfield, 87
Riggin, John Jr, 41, 47, 76
Riley, Debbie, x
Rio Grande, 131
Rock River Seminary, 5
Rocky Mountains, 202
Roeblings, Brooklyn Bridge builders, 212
Rollins
  James, 2

Jarrard Owen, 2
Rosencrans
  William, 59, 60, 103, 104, 108, 174, 175
    army severely beaten at Chickamauga, 106
    Lincoln's description, 109
    popular with his troops but disliked by Grant, 109
Rowley, William R, 9, 47, 54, 102, 126, 156, 164, 186
Runaway, Jerry, taken in by Rawlins, 98
Russell, Peter, x
Sacketts Harbor NY, Grant posted at, 16
Saint Louis MO, 14, 22, 102, 120, 175, 176, 196
  Grant posted at, 16
Salt Lake City UT, 203
San Domingo annexation failure, 219
Satartia, 89
Sauk tribe, 2
Savannah GA, 174
  Falls to Sherman, 178
Sayler's Creek, 187
Schofield, 132, 177
Scott
  Thomas A, assistant secretary of war, 38
  Winfield, 15, 122
Secession, 12
Seward, William Henry, 125

Sheean
  David, 9
    imprisoned in NY, 67
  Laura (Rawlins), 67
Shenandoah Valley, 130, 141, 150, 152, 157, 161, 162, 169, 182
Sheridan, Philip, 126, 133, 138, 146, 163, 167, 169, 182, 184, 185, 186, 187, 189, 193, 194, 215, 221
  at Missionary Ridge, 117
Sherman, William T, 57, 58, 68, 70, 78, 79, 81, 85, 86, 107, 108, 113, 115, 116, 121, 124, 125, 157, 170, 171, 182, 183, 186, 190, 194, 197, 198, 199, 208, 212, 213, 221
  attacks Meridian MS, 118
  attempt on Vicksburg, 73, 74
  attempted march on Mobile AL, 119
  at Columbia SC, 181
  death of son, 84
  defeated at Chickasaw Bayou, 69, 71
  early career, 41
  march to Atlanta, 156, 159, 160
  march to the sea, 172, 173, 174
  at Pittsburg Landing, 52
  prepares for march on Atlanta, 126, 132

replaces Smith, 41
siege of Knoxville, 118
takes Savannah, 178
Shiloh, 219
  Battle of, 52
Shreveport LA, 131
Sigel, Franz, 127, 130, 141, 152
Silver Springs MD, 157
Slavery, 10, 11
Slaves, liberated
  Crowding the roads, 83
  Employed in cotton industry, 83
  Provided with food, shelter and medical care, 61
Smith
  Bradner, 8
  C F, 29, 46
  Charles F, 32, 33
    death, 50
    Grant's former West Point instructor, 49
    Rawlins defended against drinking charges, 49
  Emily, 7, 8, 9, 180, 217
    death, 23
    photo, 8
  Giles A, 212
  Hiram, 8, 217
  Sarah, 217
    sister of Emily Smith Rawlins, 24
  Sarah Bull, 8
  William F (Baldy), 111,

William F (Baldy) (Cont.) 113, 117, 124, 132, 144, 146, 151, 168
  at Battle of Cold Harbor, 148
  ordered to seize and occupy Petersburg, 150
  relieved of duty, 158
Snyder Bluff, 73
Society of the Army of the Tennessee, 197, 198
South Anna River, 142
  Battle of, 143, 144
  map, 143
South Carolina, 12, 178
Southside Railroad, 150, 154, 155, 169, 170, 183, 184, 185, 186, 187
Spanish American War, 221
Spottsylvania, 137, 142
  Map, 137
Spottsylvania Court House, 138
Springfield IL, 21
Staff assignments, General Orders #21, 47
Stanton, Edwin M, 58, 74, 75, 79, 99, 107, 108, 162, 172, 188, 190, 203
Stevens, Isaac P, 6
Sumner, Charles, 204
Swing around the Circle, 195
Tarbell, Ida, 90
Taylor, Zachary, 15
Temperance movements, viii
Tennessee River, 40, 106,

Tennessee River (Cont.)
    110, 111
  Strategic importance, 28
Terry, Alfred, 179
Texas, 131, 190
The Hermitage, Andrew
    Jackson's home, 119
Thomas, George, 57, 58,
    106, 108, 109, 111, 116,
    121, 132, 173, 176, 221
  defeats Hood near
    Nashville, 178
  had replaced Grant after
    Shiloh, 110
Thomas, George "Slow
    Trot", 177
Thomas, Lorenzo, 61, 104
Toms River NJ, 218
Transcontinental railroad
    completion, 220
Tunnel Hill, 110, 115
Union Pacific Railroad, 200,
    202
Union Pacific Railroad
    scandal, 219
Utah, 203
Vicksburg, Fall of, 93
Vicksburg Campaign, 68, 70,
    73, 77, 79, 80, 82, 83, 84,
    85, 95, 101
  Confederate prisoners
    paroled, 93, 94
  Failures, 74
  Forty-eight day siege, 87,
    88
  Map, 70

Vicksburg MS, 66, 67, 96,
    98, 105, 219
Virginia Military Institute,
    142
Volunteer troops, Recruited
    by state governors and
    politicians, 66, 67
Wait
  Emily (Rawlins), 218
  Wesley, 218
Walden's Ridge, 109
Wallace
  Lew, 52, 54
    late arrival at Pittsburg
      Landing, 56
    refusal to abandon
      artillery, 55
Walnut Hills, 70, 71
Washburne, Elihu B, 12, 13,
    24, 25, 32, 39, 48, 61, 63,
    64, 67, 78, 101, 102, 103,
    113, 122, 123, 182, 199,
    206
Washington, George, 122
Washington DC, 161, 166,
    167, 172, 175, 176, 189,
    194, 196, 198, 203, 205,
    211, 213
  Early's advance, 157
Webster
  Colonel, 47, 56
  Noah, 8
Weldon Railroad, 150, 154,
    165, 166, 177, 179, 181,
    184
Welles, Gideon, 99

Wells, Gideon, 204, 207
West Coast, Grant posted to, 16
West Point, 195
West Point Military Academy, 14, 15, 40, 41, 42, 64, 106, 127, 218
Whiskey Ring tax evasion scandal, 219
Wilderness
  Battle of, map, 134
  Battle of the, 133, 134, 135
    staggering casualties, 137
Willard Hotel, Washington DC, 189
Wilmington NC, 150, 179
Wilson, James Harrison, viii, 64, 65, 66, 70, 71, 77, 82, 86, 88, 89, 101, 107, 110, 122, 123, 129, 133, 135, 138, 148, 177, 193, 199, 207, 209, 213, 221
  attempt on Vicksburg, 73
Wilson's Creek, 22
Winchester VA, 169
Wisconsin, 221
Wyoming Territory, 213
Yazoo Pass, 73
Yazoo River, 68, 71, 73, 79, 85, 89, 91
Young, Brigham, 203
Young's Point LA, Grant's headquarters, 70

ABOUT THE AUTHOR

The author, J. C. Ladenheim, is a student of nineteenth century American history. He has previously written about the Custer saga, the Jarrett-Palmer Transcontinental Express and several Lincoln subjects.

www.ingramcontent.com/pod-product-compliance
Lightning Source LLC
Chambersburg PA
CBHW050131170426
43197CB00011B/1796